5⁰⁰

2⁵⁰

D1222438

BARNUM IN LONDON

Also by Raymund Fitzsimons

THE BARON OF PICCADILLY: THE TRAVELS AND
ENTERTAINMENTS OF ALBERT SMITH: 1816–1860

BARNUM IN LONDON

by

RAYMUND FITZSIMONS

PUBLISHED BY

GEOFFREY BLES · LONDON

© RAYMUND FITZSIMONS, 1969

SBN: 7138 0251 0

Printed in Great Britain
by Richard Clay (The Chaucer Press) Ltd
Bungay, Suffolk

Published by
GEOFFREY BLES LTD
52 Doughty Street, London, W.C.1
36–38 Clarence Street, Sydney
353 Elizabeth Street, Melbourne
246 Queen Street, Brisbane
CML Building, King William Street, Adelaide
Lake Road, Northcote, Auckland
100 Lesmill Road, Don Mills, Ontario
P.O. Box 8879, Johannesburg
P.O. Box 834, Cape Town
P.O. Box 2800, Salisbury, Rhodesia

TO
the girl who looks more like
ANNE O'BRIEN
than any other girl I know

Yankee Doodle came to town,
    Riding on a pony;
He stuck a feather in his cap
    And called it macaroni.

A folk song popular during the American Revolutionary War. The words satirise the provincial New Englanders and were sung with derision by the British troops. But after the battle of Bunker Hill, where they forced the British to withdraw, the Americans adopted it as their own and when the British finally surrendered at Yorktown they were not a little mortified to hear the Americans playing this tune.

CONTENTS

The author is grateful to the Harvard University Press for permission to quote from *The Diaries of Benjamin Robert Haydon*, edited by Professor Willard Bissell Pope.

ILLUSTRATIONS

★ Radio Times Hulton Picture Library
† Illustrated London News

Chapter One

GOING AHEAD WITH BARNUM

ON WEDNESDAY 4 September, 1844, Albert Smith, novelist, playwright and journalist, arrived in Birmingham from London. He was at breakfast in the coffee-room at Dee's Hotel, when he was disturbed by shouts in the street. He could also hear cries coming from the yard at the rear of the hotel. In both places he was intrigued to find a crowd of three or four hundred people, apparently waiting for something wonderful to happen. The mystery was soon solved. The coach especially designed for General Tom Thumb was about to make its first appearance.

Everyone in Britain was talking about General Tom Thumb, the American dwarf. Twenty-five inches in height and perfectly formed, he was the wonder of all who had seen him. People exclaimed over the beauty of his body, the elegance of his clothes and the sauciness of his remarks. For four months he had been the rage of London. Queen Victoria had sent for him three times and lavished expensive presents on him. He had played with the Royal children. The Duke of Wellington had been chaffed by him. He had been welcomed into the houses of the nobility. At the Egyptian Hall in Piccadilly great ladies had jostled with the mob to kiss his little cheeks. Now he was touring the provinces and was appearing that week at Birmingham.

As Smith watched, two grooms, grave and important, opened the doors of the coach house with a flourish, and the Lilliputian carriage of Tom Thumb, pulled by two tiny Shetland ponies, drove out into the street. It was a perfect carriage in miniature, with a blue-and-white body no more than twenty inches high and eleven inches wide. Smith was reminded of Mercutio's description of Queen Mab's coach,

> *Her waggon-spokes made of long spinners' legs;*
> *The cover, of the wings of grasshoppers;*
> *Her traces of the smallest spider's web;*
> *Her collars of the moonshine's watery beams;*
> *Her whip of cricket's bone; the lash of film . . .*

He noticed a man holding people back from the coach; a tall man, robust and portly, with a round face, curly hair, bulbous nose, cleft chin and a mouth that seemed always to be hovering on the brink of laughter, even now as he cuffed the more intrusive boys into order. Smith recognised him as Phineas Taylor Barnum, the American showman, self-styled 'guardian' of General Tom Thumb, and he stepped out into the yard to renew his acquaintance.

After greeting Barnum, Smith asked him who had made the coach.

"Mr. Beaton of Soho," Barnum replied.

" 'Time out o' mind the fairies' coach-makers'," Smith quoted.

"Is that a fact?" said Barnum.

He suggested to Smith that they spend the next day together. He intended to go sight-seeing at Stratford and Kenilworth. He particularly wanted to visit the house where Shakespeare was born. But he told Smith that they must "go-a-head", and they certainly did. Smith saw and heard more on Thursday, 5 September, 1844, than on any other day of his life.

Smith was a well-known figure in the literary and theatrical circles of early Victorian London. He was a jovial young man, fond of drinking and good company. He had been attracted to journalism by the irregular hours and the conviviality in taverns and clubs. At all the places frequented by literary and theatrical people—the Cheshire Cheese in Fleet Street, the Cider Cellars near the stage door of the Adelphi Theatre in Maiden Lane, the

Coal Hole off the Strand and Evans' in Covent Garden—the thick-set figure of Smith was to be found. There he would stay until after midnight, when he returned to his rooms in Percy Street to spend the remainder of the night either at his desk or with a ballet girl.

Dickens delighted in Smith's Cockney exuberance, but there were others, Thackeray among them, who thought him a vulgar man with little talent except a flair for self-advertisement. And Smith was certainly fond of blowing his own trumpet. At a time when anonymity was the custom in journalism he never missed an opportunity of bringing his name before the public. He republished every scrap of his contributions to *Punch* and other periodicals under his own name, and insisted that in all advertisements for his theatrical productions his name should be prominently displayed.

His efforts to keep his name before the public did not endear him to those who believed the custom of anonymity to be a gentlemanly one. But then Smith was not a gentleman; he was a bohemian and looked like one in his check suit, gaudy neckerchief, flat broad-brimmed hat, watch chain festooned with charms and long brown hair flowing to his shoulders. Convivial, energetic and fly, he was the perfect companion for Barnum on a day out.

Smith had first met Barnum in the summer, in Robert Keeley's dressing room at the Lyceum Theatre. The twenty-eight-year-old journalist and the thirty-four-year-old showman immediately recognised in each other a kindred spirit. Smith approved of the pleasant, plausible American, who looked so essentially innocent, whose every word was accompanied by a spacious gesture and who did not talk so much as propound. He also admired the skilful way in which Barnum kept up the interest of the public in Tom Thumb. The showman's methods confirmed what he already knew—that success depended to a great extent on advertisement. On this day out, he hoped to learn more about

3

Barnum's use of ballyhoo, and he was not to be disappointed. On his return, he was to write an account of everything Barnum did and said that day.

At five o'clock in the morning, a time of day Smith had only seen when coming home from a party, Barnum knocked on his bedroom door, and by six o'clock they were seated on the box-seat of a mail-coach, whirling at a rate of twelve miles an hour over the road leading from Birmingham to Stratford, a distance of thirty miles.

After leaving Birmingham the view became picturesque, with glimpses of fine old churches and ancient villages.

"We've none of them old fixings in Amerikey," Barnum remarked. "They've no time to get old there."

"How's that?" Smith asked.

"Why, you see, a man never builds a house to last above a year or two, because he's gone-a-head in that time, and wants a bigger one. And go-a-head is our motto. Shut the firedoor, sit on the safety valve and whop the sun. We've no bonds on airth can keep us back."

"Are you all alike in America?" Smith asked.

"I reckon we are," Barnum said. "As Yankee Doodle says, the chief end of all men is to get money. So we don't swop even in any case, but strive to have the pull always. If you fail you're called a 'Do'; if you succeed you become a capitalist. There's just the same difference between a hung rebel and a crowned conqueror."

"But what does the world say to this?" Smith asked.

"Who cares what it says?" Barnum retorted. "The world's only a bugbear to frighten timid people. If you care what people say, get lots of money, and then you can make them talk as you like. They call me a humbug now. Very good. I can afford it. They won't someday. Not that I'd sooner be a humbug than anything, if it's what my experience leads me to believe it is. Humbug is, nowadays, the knack of knowing what people will

4

pay money to see or support. Anybody who's up to this is safe to be called a humbug by everybody who isn't."

To beguile the tedium of the journey, Barnum told Smith how he had humbugged the public over Joice Heth. Smith was enraptured by Barnum's reminiscences. He had long appreciated the value of advertising, and now he was being educated in the methods of humbug and ballyhoo by the greatest of masters. Barnum told his story well, and Smith's laugh rang out again and again to the chagrin of the inside passengers, who travelled in less lively company.

Joice Heth was his first show. He was running a boarding house and grocery store in New York, when one day in July, 1835, a friend, Coley Bartram, of Reading, Connecticut, called on him and gave him some interesting news. Bartram told him that he had once owned a share in an extraordinary old Negress named Joice Heth, who claimed not only to be one hundred and sixty-one years old but also to have been the nurse of no less a person than George Washington, the father of the United States of America. Furthermore, not only did she look as old as she claimed to be, but the original bill of sale for the slave was available for inspection. Bartram had sold out his interest to his partner, R. W. Lindsay of Jefferson County, Kentucky, who was now exhibiting the old lady at Philadelphia. But Lindsay, like Bartram, had not the right temperament for a showman, and now he, too, was anxious to sell out.

Barnum was interested in Bartram's news. He had thought for some time that his talents lay in show business, and he was sure he would be successful if he could only get hold of the right kind of show. So he visited the Masonic Hall in Philadelphia, where Joice Heth was being exhibited. He saw a hideous old crone lying on a couch with her legs drawn up. She could not move from this position, as both her legs were completely paralysed. Her left arm, also paralysed, lay across her breast. The fingers of this arm were half-closed, and the finger-nails were so long that they extended above her wrist. She was totally blind, and her eyes were so deeply sunken in their sockets that the eyeballs seemed to have disappeared. She had not a tooth in her head. Barnum was impressed by her appearance. So far as he could see, she might have been called a thousand years old as any other age.

Despite her disabilities, Joice was a cheerful soul and very sociable. She had been tutored to lie with such plausibility that few people doubted her story. It would seem that George Washington's celebrated regard for the truth had hardly been inculcated by his putative nurse. Joice told the audience many anecdotes about "dear little George", as she called him. She declared that she was present at his birth, and was the first person to put clothes on him. "In fact," she said, "I raised him." She claimed to have been a member of the Baptist Church for over a hundred years, and asked if any clergymen were present, as she liked to converse with them on religious topics. The sanctimonious old hypocrite ended her performance by asking the audience to gather round her couch and join with her in a session of hymn singing. All in all, Barnum thought the exhibition an extremely interesting one.

Lindsay allowed Barnum to examine the bill of sale signed by Augustine Washington, George's father, of "one negro woman, named Joice Heth, aged fifty-four years." The document bore the date 5 February, 1727, and certainly looked authentic. The paper was yellow with age, and had been folded so many times that the creases were nearly worn through. Lindsay explained why this historically important person had not been discovered years ago. It appeared that she had lain in an outhouse of John S. Bowling of Kentucky for so many years that no one knew or cared how old she was. Her extreme age had recently been brought to light by the discovery of this old bill of sale in the Record Office in Virginia, by the son of Mr. Bowling, who, while looking over some old papers, happened to notice the bill for Joice Heth. His curiosity was aroused, and further enquiries convinced him that the bill of sale applied to his father's old slave, who was, therefore, not only an incredible age but also an important historical link with the founding of the United States.

This plausible story, with its wealth of verisimilitude, together with the impressive documentary proof and the venerable appearance of Joice herself, satisfied Barnum that this was the opportunity he had been waiting for. The price of the Negress was three thousand dollars. Barnum had no more than five hundred dollars in cash, but he sold the interest in his grocery store, borrowed the rest, and so became the owner of his first slave and his first show.

Barnum plunged into the promotion of Joice Heth with the energy and aplomb that were to distinguish all his ventures in show business. To assist him, he employed a lawyer of dubious reputation named Levi Lyman, a quick-witted, smooth-talking young man, with exquisite manners. Lyman's first task was to write a dignified account of Joice Heth, putting her importance in its historical perspective. This was printed as a pamphlet and sold at the exhibition. The walls of New York were plastered with posters composed by Barnum. Shows had been advertised before, but never to this extent. Nor had advertisements ever been so adroitly worded. Barnum's advertisements for Joice Heth not only aroused the curiosity of the public but also appealed to their patriotic and religious sentiments.

NIBLO'S GARDEN—The greatest curiosity in the world, and the most interesting, particularly to Americans, is now exhibiting at the Saloon fronting on Broadway, in the building recently erected for the dioramic view, JOICE HETH, nurse to Gen. George Washington (the father of our country), who has arrived at the astonishing age of 161 years, as authentic documents will prove, and in full possession of her mental faculties. She is cheerful and healthy, although she weighs but forty-nine pounds. She relates many anecdotes of her young master;

7

she speaks also of the red-coats during the Revolutionary War, but does not appear to hold them in high estimation.

She has been visited by crowds of ladies and gentlemen, among whom were many clergymen and physicians, who have pronounced her the most ancient specimen of mortality the oldest of them has ever seen or heard of, and consider her a very great curiosity.

She has been a member of the Baptist Church for upwards of one hundred years, and seems to take great satisfaction in the conversation of ministers who visit her. She frequently sings and repeats parts of hymns and psalms.

From the very start of his career as a showman, Barnum was aware of the power of the Press, and he used it for his own ends. In return for taking out advertising space for Joice Heth, he asked for publicity for his exhibition in the editorial columns. The editors of the Rowdy Press were more than willing to accommodate him, especially as the copy he gave them made such titillating reading. "We venture to state," the *New York Daily Advertiser* said, "that since the flood, a like circumstance has not been witnessed equal to the one which is about to happen this week. Ancient or modern times furnish no parallel to the great age of this woman. Methuselah was 969 years old when he died, but nothing is said of the age of his wife. Adam attained nearly the age of his antiquated descendant. It is not unlikely that the sex in the olden time were like the daughters at the present day— unwilling to tell their age. Joice Heth is an exception; she comes out boldly, and says she is rising 160."

The *New York Sun* told of the sensation Joice had created "among the lovers of the curious and the marvellous; and a greater object of marvel and curiosity has never presented itself for their gratification". The *New York Courier and Enquirer* said there was no reason to doubt the old lady's age. "Nobody indeed would dispute it if she claimed to be five centuries, for she and the Egyptian mummy at the American Museum appear to be about of an age." Barnum must have been pleased with this necrophilic comparison, for he repeated it in the *New York Evening Star*, in which Joice's appearance was described as "very much like an Egyptian mummy just escaped from its sarcophagus". The *New York Spirit of the Times* said, "The dear old lady, after carrying on a desperate flirtation with Death, has finally jilted him. In the future editions, we shall expect to see her represented as the impersonation of time in the Primer, old Time having given her a season-ticket for life. The Wandering Jew and herself are the only two people we wot of that have been put on the free-list of this world for the season of eternity."

Joice Heth made her New York début at Niblo's Gardens on Broadway, a small summer theatre with gardens and open-air amusements. The exhibition opened with an account by Barnum of the circumstances which had led to the discovery of this astonishing old lady. He read the bill of sale, which was then passed among the audience. He questioned Joice about the birth and infancy of George Washington, and she gave him detailed answers. Members of the audience were then allowed to put questions to her, and she never failed to give them satisfactory replies. Barnum changed the subject to religious topics, on which Joice discoursed with evident delight. Now and again she broke off to sing a hymn, in which the audience joined. Sometimes one of the audience would start a hymn, which Joice and the others would take up. The audience were highly pleased by this bizarre exhibition and, for several weeks, the room was crowded at every performance.

Barnum then took Joice Heth to Boston, where he was certain her devoutness would have an especial appeal. In Boston the old Puritan practices still held sway. There was a total observation of the Sabbath from sundown on Saturday until sundown on Sunday. No theatre or other place of entertainment was allowed to open on Saturday night. On his arrival in the city, Barnum made a tour of the churches, and was pleased to find a large number of Baptist meeting-houses. He had no doubt that Joice's piety would be appreciated in Boston. As in New York, vast quantities of handbills and posters were distributed, and Joice's arrival was heralded by enthusiastic notices in the newspapers, Barnum's *quid pro quo* for taking out advertising space.

The exhibition at the Concert Hall attracted large audiences, most of whom stayed on for the hymn-singing session at the end. In Boston this part of Joice's performance became so popular that it overshadowed her reminiscences about "dear little George", and a visit to her was considered more like going to a religious service than to a show. Barnum emphasised the religious aspect of the exhibition by preaching at various meeting-houses in the city.

When the interest of Bostonians in Joice Heth began to fade Barnum looked around for some way to re-awaken their curiosity. He found his inspiration in another room at the Concert Hall, where Johann Maelzel was exhibiting his famous automaton chess player, a robot in the likeness of a Turk. A letter appeared in the leading Boston newspaper, signed "A Visitor", in which the writer claimed to have made an important discovery—namely, that Joice Heth, as exhibited, was a fraud—she was not a human being but a robot! "What purports to be a remarkable old woman," the writer continued, "is simply a curiously constructed automaton, made of whalebone, india-rubber, and numberless springs ingeniously put together, and made to move at the slightest touch, according to the will of the operator. The exhibitor is a ventriloquist, and all the conversations apparently held with the ancient lady are purely imaginary, so far as she is concerned, for the answers and incidents purporting to be given and related by her, are merely the ventriloquial voice of the exhibitor."

Barnum was, of course, the writer of this letter, which succeeded in making Joice Heth more curious and interesting than before. Maelzel's exhibition of automatons gave substance to these revelations. Those who had not visited Joice Heth were now anxious to see this marvellous automaton, and those who had seen her now wanted to take a second look to discover how they had been deceived, with the result that every performance was crowded for a further two weeks.

Barnum returned with Joice to New York for another successful season at Niblo's Gardens, but his good fortune did not last, for Joice sickened, and after a short illness she died on 19 February, 1836.

As the mail coach approached the village of Henley-in-Arden, heavy rain began to fall, but Barnum and Smith were in such good humour that they laughed at the weather. The coachman asked Barnum if he was afraid of catching a cold, and Barnum replied that he was not at all afraid, for the horses went too slow to catch anything.

The village of Henley was four miles from Stratford, but the fame of the Bard of Avon had evidently carried that far, for they noticed a sign over a barber's shop, "Shakespeare—hairdresser—a good shave for a penny". This gave rise to some speculation on Barnum's part.

"Now if that barber was just to write a play," he said, "it wouldn't be thought anything of, however good it was, till he'd been dead no end of years. You talk a good deal about your Shakespeare being the pride of England, but I can see nobody knew or cared a cent about him while he was alive, or else you'd have known more of him now. If he'd been a living author, and I'd had my exhibition, I'd have backed General Tom Thumb to have shut him up in a week." He told Smith that even Joice Heth dead had proved to be vastly more interesting than Joice Heth living.

A surgeon who had visited the exhibition had extracted a promise from Barnum that he be allowed to conduct a post-mortem on Joice, in the unlikely, as it seemed then, event of her death. There was great excitement in the medical world when the time and place of the portmortem was announced. In New York doctors argued about the probable state of the vascular system in a person presumed to be so old, while in Boston the doctors marvelled at the credulity of their New York colleagues, knowing as they did that the examination would reveal nothing more than whale bone, india rubber and metal springs.

High prices were paid to be present at the portmortem. The leading medical men in America assisted at it. Clergymen and newspaper reporters were there. Barnum and Lyman were also in attendance. The doctor who was to conduct the examination gave a lecture beforehand on the vast extent of ossification of the arteries that would be met with. But he met with nothing of the kind. Far from being one hundred and sixty-one years old, he estimated that Joice Heth must have been between seventy-five and eighty at the time of her death.

The entire Rowdy Press of New York now turned its attention to Barnum. British visitors to America were affronted by the Rowdy Press, which had no counterpart in their own country. In Britain newspapers were read mainly by the upper and middle classes, and tended to be responsible and conservative. In America, however, the newspaper was the standard reading of the great majority of the people, who, in their busy lives, had no time for books, and who, if they did not find their reading in a newspaper, did not read at all. To attract readers, the New York papers vied with each other in sensationalism. Their main weapon was the libellous personal attack. No one was spared, from the President downwards. Stories, no matter how damaging, were never checked for accuracy, and the more titillating, ribald or nasty the details, the greater prominence was given. The Rowdy Press was a frightful organ, and Dickens, who had suffered at its hands, made it the target for some of the most biting satire in *Martin Chuzzlewit*. On his arrival in New York, the first sound heard by Martin Chuzzlewit was the shouting of the newsboys.

" 'Here's this morning's New York Sewer!' cried one. 'Here's this morning's New York Stabber! Here's the New York Family Spy! Here's the New York Private Listener! Here's the New York Peeper! Here's the New York Plunderer! Here's the New York Keyhole Reporter! Here's the New York Rowdy Journal! Here's all the New York papers! Here's full particulars of the patriotic loco-foco movement yesterday, in which the whigs was so chawed up; and the last Alabama gouging case; and the interesting Arkansas dooel with Bowie knives; and all the Political, Commercial, and Fashionable News! Here they are! Here's the papers!' "

The entire Rowdy Press of New York now turned its artillery on Barnum. The *New York Sun* opened fire with an account of the postmortem and the findings of the doctor, under the headline DISSECTION OF JOICE HETH—PRECIOUS HUMBUG EXPOSED.

Barnum protested that he had hired Joice Heth in good faith, relying upon her appearance and the bill of sale as evidence of the truth of her story. When people said he must have been over-credulous he replied that so must many others, for when Joice was living he had never met with more than half a dozen people out of the thousands who visited her who doubted her age. Moreover, if Joice were an imposter, how was she familiar with minute details of the Washington family that had not been known to anyone? And, indeed, many people who had seen her alive were astonished by the accounts they read of the postmortem, and said there must have been a mistake. Some said she could not be less than a hundred, while others believed she was quite as old as she had claimed to be. While the public were thus confused, Barnum called on James Gordon Bennett, editor of the *New York Herald*.

Of all the rowdy newspapers in New York, the *New York Herald* was the rowdiest. Bennett was just beginning his tempestuous voyage in the seas of sensational journalism. He became so notorious that he was an outcast from decent society for most of his life. He served as a model for Colonel Diver, editor of the "New York Rowdy Journal", a character in *Martin Chuzzlewit*, who, in his "perfect understanding of public sentiment", cared nothing for what anyone thought about him. "His high-spiced wares were made to sell, and they sold," Dickens wrote; "and his thousands of readers could as rationally charge their delight in filth upon him, as a glutton can shift upon his cook the responsibility of his beastly excess. Nothing would have delighted him more than to be told that no such man as he could walk in high success the streets of any other country in the world: for that would only have been a logical assurance to him of the correct adaptation of his labours to the prevailing taste, and of being strictly and peculiarly a national feature of America."

In Barnum, Bennett recognised another who had a "perfect understanding of public sentiment". He welcomed the story Barnum had to tell him, especially as it gave him the opportunity to score off his rival, the *New York Sun*, which had scooped his newspaper with its account of the findings of the portmortem. Barnum now told Bennett that the portmortem had been a hoax, and that Joice Heth was, at that moment, being exhibited in Connecticut, and that the body that had been dissected as hers was that of an old Negress named Aunt Nelly, who had recently died in Harlem. This story appeared in the *New York Herald* on 27 February, under the headline JOICE HETH IS NOT DEAD.

On Wednesday last as we learn from the best authority, she was living at Hebron, in Connecticut, where she then was. The subject on which Doctor Rogers and the Medical Faculty of Barclay Street have been exercising their knife and their ingenuity, is the remains of a respectable old Negress called Aunt Nelly, who has lived many years in a small house by herself, in Harlem, belonging to Mr. Clarke. She is, as Dr. Rogers sagely discovers, and Dr. Locke his colleague accurately records, only eighty years of age. Aunt Nelly before her death complained of old age and infirmity. She was otherwise in good spirits. The recent winter, however, has been very severe, and so she gave up the ghost a few days ago.

Some person in this city . . . resolved, as soon as he heard from a friend of the death of poor Aunt Nelly, to send her body into the city, and contrive to pass her off upon the Medical Faculty for the veritable Joice Heth. The trick took. Several of the hoaxed went, looked, wondered, and held up their hands in astonishment. Her death was announced in the Sun, and a postmortem examination prepared. The public swallowed the pill. Aunt Nelly, neglected, unknown, unpitied when alive, became an object of deep science and deeper investigation when she died. She looked as old and ugly as Joice herself, and in that respect answered the thing exactly.

Such is the true version of the hoax, as given us by good authority . . .

The public were already confused over the truth about Joice Heth and, with this newspaper report, Barnum was to confuse them even more. Many of those who read this story believed it. They were sure the old lady they had paid to see was considerably more than eighty, and now the *New York Herald* had made the matter perfectly clear. The Rowdy Press had been firing at Barnum, but now he had smartly manoeuvred them into shooting at one another. The *New York Sun*, which had been the first to print an account of the postmortem, insisted that this had not been a hoax. The *New York Herald* insisted that it was, and even laid a wager of several hundred dollars that Joice was alive and being exhibited in Connecticut. When Bennett found that he was the one who had been hoaxed, he cried all the louder that he was right, and published forged statements in the *New York Herald*, written and signed by persons living in Harlem who had known Aunt Nelly. Barnum observed that "seldom had vastly more important matters been so widely discussed", but the controversy served his purpose by keeping the public in a state of confusion.

In September, when the echoes of the Joice Heth affair were dying away, Bennett met Lyman in the street and took him to task over Barnum having made a fool of him. Lyman told

Bennett that the story of Aunt Nelly given to him by Barnum had been meant as a harmless joke, but as a recompense he would reveal exclusively to him the *true* facts about Joice Heth. Lyman told him that Barnum had bought an old Negress, extracted all her teeth and taught her the Washington story. Lyman's revelations, filled out and embellished by Bennett himself, ran to several columns in two issues of the *New York Herald*. The first instalment began:

A full and accurate account of the hoax, perpetrated by Joice Heth and her friends, upon the cities of Philadelphia, New York, and Boston, and particularly upon the medical faculty of each, will be one of the most interesting histories of this singular exposition of human ingenuity on the one side—and human credulity on the other . . . *There can be no mistake about the facts related*, because we have taken them down from the lips of the very individual who originated and carried into effect this most stupendous hoax, illustrative of the accuracy of medical science, the skill of medical men, and the general good-nature and credulity of the public.

Barnum made no attempt to deny this story, even though he stood accused of deceiving the public. His first effort as a showman had taught him two lessons about the value of publicity. He had learnt the first one earlier in the year, when he discovered that the controversy over Joice Heth served his purpose as a showman by keeping his name before the public. Now he had learnt the second lesson, the one that was to set him on a pinnacle above any other showman who ever lived. Barnum was the first man to appreciate the supreme, the ultimate value of publicity: that any kind of publicity was better than none, and that it did not matter what the newspapers said about you so long as they mentioned your name.

Twenty minutes after leaving Henley-in-Arden, Barnum and Smith alighted at the Red Horse Hotel in Stratford-upon-Avon.

While they waited for their breakfast, Smith read aloud from Washington Irving's *Sketch Book*, a copy of which was kept in the parlour of the inn. The chapter on Stratford was well thumbed, for visitors had no better guide to introduce them to Shakespeare's birth and burial place.

"My first visit," Smith read, "was to the house where Shakespeare was born, and where, according to tradition, he was brought up to his father's craft of wool-combing. It is a small, mean-looking edifice of wood and plaster, a true nestling place of genius, which seems to delight in hatching its off-spring in by-corners. The walls of its squalid chambers are covered with names and inscriptions in every language, by pilgrims of all nations, ranks and conditions, from the prince to the peasant, and present a simple but striking instance of the spontaneous and universal homage of mankind to the great poet of nature."

After breakfast they visited Shakespeare's house, where an old lady showed them a collection of dubious relics, which included the shattered stock of the match-lock used by Shakespeare on his poaching exploit in Sir Thomas Lucy's estate, the sword he had worn when he played Hamlet and the identical lantern with which Friar Laurence had discovered Romeo and Juliet at the tomb. Barnum pointed to a portrait on the wall.

"I see you've got pictures here, ma'am," he said.

"Yes, sir," the old lady replied, "that is the only one: a likeness of Shakespeare."

"Very good," Barnum said, "it wants a companion. I'll send you a portrait of the General from Birmingham, and you can hang it up too, you know, the other side."

They examined the famous names in the visitors' book. The worn appearance of the page on which Dickens had put his autograph was proof of the popularity of the great Boz. Barnum signed himself 'P. T. Barnum, U.S., Guardian of General Tom Thumb'. As they left, he gave the old lady a pile of the miniature visiting cards Tom Thumb distributed at his performances, and asked her to inform all visitors to Shakespeare's house that the dwarf was to be seen every day at Birmingham.

As Washington Irving had remarked, only a few paces separated Shakespeare's birthplace from his grave, and Barnum and Smith strolled over to the chancel of the church, where the poet lay buried. The sexton gave them the visitors' book to sign, and Barnum asked if Dickens's name was in it. "No sir," the sexton replied, with a heavy sigh, "it is not." This was evidently a sore point. The house, with its wealth of relics, had always had more visitors than the church, and now it had this added attraction.

"A flat stone marks the spot where the bard is buried," Irving wrote. "There are four lines inscribed on it, said to have been written by himself, and which have something in them extremely awful. If they are indeed his own, they show that solicitude about the quiet of the grave which seems natural to fine sensibilities and thoughtful minds.

> *Good friend, for Jesus' sake forbeare*
> *To dig the dust enclosed here*
> *Blessed be he that spares these stones*
> *And curst be he that moves my bones."*

Barnum placed one of Tom Thumb's visiting cards on the tomb by way of an advertisement, and then returned with Smith to the inn, where they ordered a fly for Warwick.

The distance between Stratford and Warwick is fourteen miles and, as they drove along, the conversation turned again to show business. Smith was beginning to notice that Barnum's only interest that day, on what he called his "sight-seeing tour", was to find some attractions to send back to America. He recalled that Barnum had already sent over a group of Lancashire bell-ringers, and he asked if they were a success in New York.

"Oh, yes—I should think so," Barnum said. "They were Lankayshire lads you had in London; but I called them the Swiss Youths. I engaged them here, and I said, 'Now let your mustachios grow, and you'll be downright foreigners by the time you get to America.'—'But,' says they, speaking in their country fashion, which was uncommon grating, to be sure, 'how'll they take us to be Swiss?'—'Well,' says I, 'if you always speak as you're doing now, the devil himself won't understand you.' And sure enough, when they got there, nobody did; but they drew a heap of money to the Museum.''

"But wouldn't they have been an attraction as Lancashire bell-ringers?" Smith asked.

"I reckon they would," Barnum replied. "But you see the more foreign a show is the more folk like it. That's why I called General Tom Thumb an Englishman in New York and an American over here. The longer the distance, and the more trouble and expense you say you had getting a show, the more folk appreciate seeing it. A man has the right to take in the public if he can. He's fighting single-handed against all creation, and it's the greatest credit to him if he whops them, for they are long odds." And he told Smith the story of Signor Vivalla.

Although he had informed the public that Joice Heth had been "put on the free-list of this world for the season of eternity", he himself was only too conscious of her mortality and of the need to find another exhibit before she went to claim whatever eternal reward was merited by *soi-disant* nurses of George Washington. Shortly before Joice's death he saw a performance of juggling by a grimy little Italian, who had just arrived in America. Some of the tricks were new to him, and he felt that, given the right publicity, the juggler could bring in the crowds. Barnum engaged him on three conditions. First, that he agreed to call himself Signor Vivalla and second, that he would never admit to speaking English, a language the Italian spoke well, for although he had recently emigrated to America, he had not come directly from Italy but from Britain, where he had spent some years performing at country fairs. Barnum imposed these conditions because he believed his countrymen would prefer a foreign juggler to a native one, especially if he could persuade them that he had gone to great trouble and expense to import him. The name, Signor Vivalla, not only signified an Italian but a distinguished one at that. The third condition, and by no means the least, was that the little Italian agreed to wash himself at more regular intervals than he had been in the habit of doing.

Next, as in the case of Joice Heth, Barnum turned his attention to the Press. A news item appeared in a New York paper concerning the arrival from Italy of Signor Vivalla, a juggler of extraordinary skill. Barnum sent copies of this issue to all the theatre managers in New York. The first manager to be offered the services of the eminent Italian at first refused, on the understandable grounds that he had seen many performances of the same kind. Barnum then asked him if he thought he would have brought Signor Vivalla to America unless he had been certain that he was the greatest juggler in Europe. This argument impressed the manager and he booked Signor Vivalla for a week.

Barnum flooded New York with posters announcing the first appearance in America of "the renowned and extraordinary Italian artist, Signor Vivalla". On the opening night, the theatre was packed. The little Italian, who had been grateful for the small knot of people who gathered to watch him in English marketplaces, had never had such an audience. To stress that the juggler was an exotic visitor, Barnum appeared on the stage with him to announce each trick. Through Barnum the distinguished Italian apologised to the audience for his inability to speak their language. The need for an interpreter gave a glamour to the juggling act, which gratified the audience. This, together with their desire to show a foreigner what a hospitable people they were, caused them to give tremendous applause to tricks that had been performed many times all over America. At the end of the evening Barnum again addressed the audience in Signor Vivalla's name,

Phineas Taylor Barnum

Tom Thumb posing between two guardsmen

conveying to them the Italian's gratitude and his felicitations to the great American nation.

After the New York engagement Barnum took Signor Vivalla on tour. At Boston he had a successful week, but at Philadelphia disaster struck. On the first night the performance was rapturously received, but on the second night distinct sounds of disapproval were heard from the pit. These came from a member of the audience named Roberts, who was himself a juggler. Roberts shouted that not one of the tricks was new, and that he could do all that Vivalla could. As Barnum and Roberts argued, Barnum was quick to notice that the sympathy of the audience was going to the American juggler. Patriotic feeling was overcoming their regard for a foreign entertainer, however distinguished. Barnum realised that unless he worked quickly, the reputation of Signor Vivalla would be tarnished for ever. Immediately after the performance he saw Roberts privately and came to an arrangement with him. The next morning an advertisement appeared in all the Philadelphia papers headed ONE THOUSAND DOLLARS REWARD, and stating that Signor Vivalla would pay that sum to any man who could repeat his tricks in public. Roberts accepted the challenge.

The coming trial of skill was given great prominence in the Press. All the newspapers declared that Roberts, being an American, could beat any foreigner. Roberts gave an interview to reporters, where he stated that if he won he would give a portion of the thousand dollars to charity. On the night of the contest the theatre was crowded. Barnum had found out which tricks Roberts could do and which he could not. Roberts, of course, was to be beaten, but the contest was to be kept up as long as possible. For a time the jugglers seemed evenly matched. Each of Roberts's victories was greeted with cheers and a chorus of 'Yankee Doodle'. The contest had lasted forty minutes before he came forward and acknowledged defeat. He had failed to equal Signor Vivalla's feat of spinning two plates in the air at once.

Roberts announced to the audience that he was handicapped that
night by a sprained wrist. Moreover, there were tricks he could
do which the Italian could not. He challenged Vivalla to equal *his*
tricks at any time and place he pleased for a wager of five hundred
dollars. Vivalla accepted the challenge and named the following
Tuesday night at the same theatre. The antagonists then gave each
other a contemptuous look and withdrew at opposite sides of the
stage. The return contest attracted a great crowd, and Signor
Vivalla was again the winner. Similar trials of skill between
Vivalla and Roberts took place in New York and elsewhere, but
such contests could not go on indefinitely without the public
becoming suspicious, so Barnum and Vivalla set off alone for a
tour of New England.

Barnum and Smith found the town of Warwick in holiday
mood, for it was the day of the races. After lunch at the Warwick
Arms they walked to the lodge of the castle and knocked on the
gate. It was opened by an old porter, who asked them if they
wanted to see round the castle. "Well, now," Barnum said
amiably, "what the devil do you think we came and knocked
here for, if we didn't?" The old man was affronted and let them
in without another word.

They strolled up the great drive to the entrance of the inhabited
wing, where they were received by a dignified butler, who told
them that as the family were away he would show them round
the apartments for the small sum of half a crown each. He took
them through the Red Drawing Room, the Cedar Drawing
Room, the Gilt Room, the State Bedroom, Lady Warwick's
Boudoir, the Compass Room and the Chapel. There was a great
deal to see, and Barnum wanted to buy most of it for his American
Museum. He particularly fancied the portraits of Elizabeth and
Leicester, and a pair of horns of a gigantic elk, dug up from a bog
in Ireland.

As they left this part of the castle the butler placed them in the charge of another guide, who took them to the top of Guy's Tower. The view was enchanting, and they could see far below them the white tents on the green racecourse fluttering in the sun and wind. All the way up the tower there were cunningly placed slits in the wall for shooting arrows. Smith remarked that Warwick Castle, in its day, must have been a tough place to attack, and Barnum admitted that only America could have taken it.

When they came down from Guy's Tower, another guide, who looked old enough to have known Guy himself, hobbled across the grounds to show them the Warwick Vase. He mounted a rostrum at the side of the vase, and began a set speech so interminable that they left him in the middle of his oration, and went back down the drive to the lodge. They were under the impression that they had seen everything, but as they passed the lodge on the way out, the old porter whom Barnum had offended told them that the most curious relics connected with the legendary Guy were to be seen in his house.

They entered the lodge, and the old man, now very much on his dignity with Barnum, showed them the armour Guy had worn when he fought and killed the Great Dun Cow. The sword, shield, helmet and breastplate were all a colossal size. Together they weighed nearly six hundred pounds. The horse armour would have fitted an elephant. He also showed them Guy's Porridge Pot, a cauldron two or three feet across, which would hold at least seventy gallons; and Guy's Flesh-Fork, a metal instrument the size of a farmer's hay fork; and a rib of the Great Dun Cow, a bone so large that it could have come only from a mastodon.

"I say, old fellow," Barnum interrupted, "I should reckon you'd told these lies so often that you believe them to be true. What'll you take now for the lot?"

The old man was astounded at the impudence of the tall genial American.

"They are not for sale," he said angrily, "they are heirlooms in the family."

"Just as you like," Barnum replied, "but I'll get up a better set than these within six months at my Museum, and I'll swear mine are the real originals, and bust up your show in no time."

The old retainer's feelings were so hurt that he could not bring himself to speak, even when they each gave him two shillings on leaving.

The arrangement of four guides for Warwick Castle, each expecting to be tipped, grieved Barnum.

"I don't mind the coin," he said, "but it's too much, and don't look nat'ral anywhere out of St. Paul's Cathedral, and your other expensive religious peep-shows. We whop you to smash as a free and intelligent nation in that, I reckon."

A ten-minute walk brought them from Warwick Castle to the racecourse, and among the sideshows, Barnum was in his glory; in fact, he never looked at the races. The sideshows were lined along one side of the course for a distance of a quarter of a mile. Barnum and Smith stopped outside a small tent, which had a large pictorial poster depicting Ojibbeway Indians, albino girls, learned pigs, giantesses and enormous snakes, only a few, it appeared, of the many attractions to be seen within.

"Ask the opinion of the respectable company who are now leaving the tent," the showman shouted.

They followed his advice and, being told it was "uncommon good", they paid their threepence, although Barnum fought hard to be classed with the 'servants and working-people' at a penny.

When the tent was full the showman brought on a gentle Negro with some feathers in his hair, who passed as an Ojibbeway Indian among the lads and lasses of Warwickshire, and with whom, to Smith's astonishment, Barnum was acquainted. While Smith was admiring the two giantesses, each over seven feet in height, Barnum stooped down beside one of them and lifted the hem of her dress, which reached to the floor. The young lady took exception to this liberty, and laid him on the floor with one blow from her brawny hand, but not before he had discovered that she was standing on a pedestal eighteen inches high.

The news that Barnum was on the racecourse carried quickly along the line of shows, and when he left the tent a crowd of showmen surrounded him, all disputing the merits of Tom Thumb.

"Now I've seen Tom Thumb," said one of the showmen, "and he's a fine little squab, but the only 'vantage he's got is he can *chaff* so well. He chaffs like a man; but I can learn Dick Swift in two months so that he can chaff Tom Thumb crazy."

"Never mind," said another, "I've got a chap training what you none on you knows, what'll beat all the thumbs on your grapplers."

"No, he can't," said a third, "for Tom Thumb has got the name, and you all know the name's everything. Tom Thumb couldn't never shine, even in my 'van, 'longside of a dozen dwarfs I knows, if this Yankee hadn't bamboozled our Queen—God bless her—by getting him afore her half a dozen times."

"I know a dwarf in Lambeth," said the first showman, "that Tom Thumb could put in his pocket, only she can't chaff like the General."

"No," Barnum replied, "I reckon not. They're precious few that can. The General can chaff the sky yellow when he pleases. He's a regular screamer. But who's this dwarf—Emma Pattle?"

Smith noticed that Barnum seemed to know about every dwarf in Britain.

"That's her," the showman said.

"Rubbish," Barnum said. "Tom Thumb put *her* in his pocket! Stuff! None of them can touch him. They hire children that can't walk and ain't weaned, and put them into top-boots and cocked hats to make generals, but it's no go."

He changed the subject abruptly. "Now look here, do you know a good giant who'd go out to Amerikey for my Museum?"

"Why, you've got one," the showman said.

"Ah, but I want another to get up an opposition against myself; don't you see?"

"There's Bob Hayes," the showman said, "he's over seven feet, but he's got his own caravans, and it wouldn't be worth his while. I don't know where he is, too."

"He's in Leicestershire," said Barnum, who was evidently acquainted with all his movements.

The showman advised him to approach the giant in the last caravan along the rank. As they walked down the line of shows, Smith remarked to Barnum that he seemed very well briefed about all the giants in the world.

"The giants know me," Barnum said. "The last one I had broke his engagement and set up against me, but I put him in prison, and there he is, safely kept until I want him."

They reached the giant's caravan, and Barnum swiftly concluded his arrangements with him. The giant agreed to travel to New York in the *Washington*, which was to sail in a few days' time from Liverpool. He was to have a salary of seven pounds a week and a military uniform to exhibit in.

Smith asked Barnum what other attractions he had sent over to America.

"I've sent them over the court suit that the General wore before her Majesty," Barnum said.

"Didn't I see the General wearing it yesterday at Birmingham?" Smith asked.

"So you did," Barnum replied, "but the one I've sent over is so like it that even the tailor couldn't tell which was which. They'll crowd to see it in New York. There's nothing like a bit of state or aristocracy to catch a Yankee, with all his talk."

They returned to the Warwick Arms, where they hired another fly, and set off for Coventry, intending to pause at Kenilworth Castle on the way. Barnum remarked on the absence of a mermaid among the sideshows at Warwick Fair. Smith told him that mermaids had been out of fashion for twenty years and that nowadays not even the simplest farm lad would be taken in by these gruesome objects constructed from the top part of a monkey and the bottom part of a fish. Barnum laughed and told him the story of the Feejee Mermaid.

Early in the summer of 1842 Moses Kimball, a Boston showman, called on Barnum and showed him what he claimed to be a mermaid. It was an ugly specimen about three feet long, the combination of the upper part of a monkey and the lower part of a fish. It was so well made that no eye could detect the join. The mouth was open, the tail was turned over, the arms were thrown up, which, all in all, gave it the appearance of having died in great agony.

The Feejee Mermaid—the name was Barnum's invention—had a long history. It was manufactured by a Japanese fisherman, who said he had caught the creature alive in his net, but that it had died shortly after being taken out of the water. The exhibition of the sea-monster paid well in Japan, but what paid better was the fisherman's assertion that the half-human fish had spoken during the few minutes it had lived out of the water, and had predicted a certain number of years of fertility to be followed by a fatal epidemic, the only remedy against which would be a picture of the prophet. The pictures of the mermaid enjoyed a tremendous sale.

Many years later the mermaid turned up in Batavia. There it was acquired by an American captain, who, believing it would astonish others as much as it astonished him, appropriated six thousand dollars of the ship's money to buy it and, leaving the ship in charge of the mate, came to London. In 1822 the mermaid was exhibited at the Egyptian Hall in Piccadilly, where for some weeks it attracted crowds of three hundred people a day. Its ownership gave rise to litigation, and this is the only recorded instance in British law where a judge has been called upon to decide the fate of a mermaid. The captain eventually returned to Boston, where his employer forced him to serve on his ship without pay until he had made up the money he had stolen. He preserved his curiosity with care and, when he died, he left it to his son, who sold it to Moses Kimball, proprietor of the Boston Museum.

Barnum was interested in the mermaid and asked a naturalist to examine it. The naturalist found that the spine of the fish continued in a straight and apparently unbroken line to the base of the skull. He had no idea how the mermaid had been manufactured. "Then, why do you suppose it is manufactured?" Barnum asked him. "Because I don't believe in mermaids," the naturalist replied. "That is no reason at all," Barnum said. "I'll believe in mermaids and hire it."

Having converted himself to a belief in mermaids, Barnum then set about converting the public. A letter appeared in the *New York Herald*, dated and posted from Montgomery, Alabama, giving the news of the day and the state of the crops. Among the items of news mentioned in the letter was one about a certain Dr. Griffin, of the Lyceum of Natural History in London, recently arrived from Pernambuco, who had in his possession a most remarkable curiosity, being nothing less than a mermaid taken among the Feejee Islands, and preserved in China, where the doctor had bought it at a high figure.

A week later a similar letter, dated and posted in Charleston, South Carolina, appeared in another New York paper. This was followed by a third letter, dated and posted in Washington, published in yet another New York paper, but, in addition, this letter expressed the hope that the people of New York be granted a look at this extraordinary curiosity before Dr. Griffin sailed for Britain. All these letters had been written by Barnum and forwarded to friends in the South, with instructions to post each of them on the date given.

A few days after the last letter was published, Levi Lyman, the smooth-talking lawyer who had assisted Barnum in the promotion of Joice Heth, registered at the leading hotel in Philadelphia as Dr. Griffin from Pernambuco, bound for London. The doctor, dignified yet friendly, was obviously a gentleman. After paying his bill, on the afternoon before he left for New York, he thanked the landlord for looking after him so well, and to show his appreciation he invited him to step into his room, where he would let him see a wonderful curiosity. The landlord was astonished at the sight of the mermaid and begged the doctor to allow him to bring some friends to see this marvellous specimen. The doctor courteously agreed, and suggested to the landlord that he include some newspaper editors among the audience.

The next day the Philadelphia newspapers were filled with stories about the mermaid, and some of these accounts were repeated in the New York papers. Lyman then returned to New York. He registered as Dr. Griffin at the Pacific Hotel and let it be known that the mermaid was in town. Reporters rushed to the hotel to see the mermaid, and Dr. Griffin graciously permitted them to satisfy their interest. The following day all the New York papers carried stories about the mermaid.

Meanwhile Barnum continued to work secretly. For the moment he did not want his connection with the mermaid to be known, in case the public, remembering Joice Heth, might suspect a hoax. He printed ten thousand leaflets illustrated with engravings of mermaids. But these mermaids were totally unlike the repulsive object in Dr. Griffin's possession. These were seductive mermaids, some reclining on rocks, others combing their hair; dazzlingly, indisputably feminine, they were destined to make the heart of every man in New York beat faster. The leaflet set out to prove the authenticity of these marvellous creatures, but nowhere did it say that these were engravings of Dr. Griffin's mermaid. Barnum allowed the public to make that deduction themselves.

As mermaids were in the news, the papers were delighted to print Barnum's learned commentary on them together with the engravings. In addition to this, Barnum distributed his leaflets throughout the city. New York was soon in the grip of a mermaid mania, and when the madness was at its height an advertisement appeared all over the town.

THE MERMAID—The public are respectfully informed that, in accordance with numerous and urgent solicitations from scientific gentlemen in this city, Dr. J. Griffin, proprietor of the Mermaid, recently arrived from Pernambuco, S.A., has consented to exhibit it to the public, *positively for one week only*! For this purpose he has procured the spacious saloon known as Concert Hall, 404 Broadway, which will open on Monday, August 8, 1842, and will positively close on Saturday the 13th inst.

The animal was taken near the Feejee Islands, and purchased for a large sum by the present proprietor, for the Lyceum of Natural History in London, and is exhibited for this short period more for the gratification of the public than for gain . . .

Great crowds visited the Concert Hall, where Lyman as Dr. Griffin exhibited the mermaid with great dignity. He lectured his audiences on the marvels of nature in general and mermaids in particular. At one session a gentleman protested, "But I lived for three years in the Feejee Islands and never heard of a mermaid." "There is no accounting for ignorance," said the imperturbable Lyman. But there were times during the exhibition when even Lyman's composure almost deserted him. Some men, beguiled by the engravings of mermaids they had seen in the newspapers, were naturally disappointed when they saw a small, black dried-up creature with a terrifying countenance, and Lyman was sometimes the centre of a nasty scene.

After a week at the Concert Hall the mermaid was advertised to be seen at Barnum's American Museum 'without extra charge'. A great banner, depicting a mermaid eighteen feet long, streamed in front of the Museum. Lyman, walking down Broadway to give his first lecture, saw the banner, and his nerve failed him. He rushed into Barnum's office and told him that this time he had gone too far. No member of the public would be satisfied with their mermaid after seeing the one on the banner. He refused to give his lecture unless the banner was removed. Barnum argued that the banner was only to catch the eye, and that no one really expected to see a mermaid that size. But Lyman could not be talked round. Barnum could not do without 'Dr. Griffin', so he took down the banner. Although Lyman still had some trouble with frustrated males, the audiences, for the most part, seemed content with what they saw: not every man cared to make it known that his reasons for coming to view the mermaid were other than scientific.

The stones of Kenilworth Castle glowed in the sunlight. Within the enclosure of the ruins, a group had assembled round a young lady who was reading aloud from Sir Walter Scott's romance. Their rapt attention showed that they had restored and peopled every part of the old castle, and that Amy Robsart, Elizabeth and Leicester were living out again the drama of their lives.

"I took above a hundred pounds a day in shillings for the General at Birmingham and Manchester," said Barnum, whose thoughts had not strayed for one instant from the present. "Pretty steep business, wasn't it?"

They walked back to their carriage. "It was all a chance, though," he continued. "I brought over a thousand pounds from New York with Tom Thumb, and I spent every farthing of it in your country making him go, and all with Englishmen. The *Liverpool Chronicle* folks know it, I reckon, for they were the first I saw. The General didn't draw though at first. It wasn't till I got him to London, in Lord Talbot's private house, that he did anything. And then I made no charge; but I put a plate on the table with a sovereign or two in it; and they took the hint first rate."

The journey from Warwick to Coventry was taking them through some of the loveliest country in Britain. Smith told Barnum an anecdote of a dispute between two commercial travellers over which was the most beautiful ride in England, each claiming he knew the best. A bet was made, and each man wrote on a slip of paper the name of his favourite journey. When the slips were read it was found that one of the men had written "from Warwick to Coventry", and the other "from Coventry to Warwick."

"Is that a fact!" Barnum exclaimed.

At Coventry their carriage crossed the railway bridge, and set them down on the corner, where an effigy of Peeping Tom was shown in the act of looking out upon Lady Godiva.

At St. Mary's Hall Barnum bought "The Happy Family", two hundred different breeds of animals and birds, all living in harmony in one cage. This cost him five hundred pounds. He also hired the proprietor to accompany the exhibition to New York, and settled that they were to sail with the giant.

It was now nine o'clock at night, and Barnum and Smith made their way to the railway station. This day that Smith had spent with Barnum was to change the course of his life. He, too, was to turn his talents to show business, and by using Barnum's methods he became one of the greatest showmen in Britain.★

At a quarter past nine they left Coventry by train, and arrived back in Birmingham at ten. Smith was completely exhausted, having visited in one day Stratford, Warwick Castle, Kenilworth and Coventry, by means of mail coach, phaëton, fly, railway and his own legs. The events of the day and the stories Barnum had told him tumbled through his mind in a confused sequence. He saw Joice Heth in Shakespeare's house and the Feejee Mermaid at Warwick Fair, Signor Vivalla juggled among the ruins of Kenilworth and Tom Thumb acted as their guide at Warwick Castle. When Smith expressed his fatigue at supper Barnum said, "Well, I don't know what you call work in England, but if you don't make thirty hours out of the twenty-four in Amerikey, I don't know where you'd be at the year's end. If a man can't beat himself in running he'll never go-a-head; and if he don't go-a-head he's done."

★ See *The Baron of Piccadilly* by the same author.

Chapter Two

YANKEE DOODLE AND HIS UNNAT'RAL
OLD PARENT

BARNUM HAD been 'going ahead' in Britain ever since he had
arrived, seven months earlier, with his dwarf, General Tom
Thumb. The success of Tom Thumb in America had convinced
Barnum that if he were to exploit the dwarf to the full he must
seek a wider field of operation. When he decided to bring Tom
Thumb to Europe he had no idea how the dwarf would be
received. "Much as I hoped for success," he wrote, "in my most
sanguine moods, I could not anticipate the half of what was in
store for me; I did not foresee or dream that I was shortly to be
brought in close contact with kings, queens, lords and illustrious
commoners, and that such association, by means of my exhibition,
would afterwards introduce me to the great public and the public's
money, which was to fill my coffers."

The British themselves would have been equally astonished had
they known that an American, of all people, was to enjoy so
spectacular a success in their country. When Barnum came to
London, in 1844, the British attitude towards America was one of
condescension. They saw the Americans as boorish citizens of a
fourth-rate country and they never neglected an opportunity to
say so. At the time of Barnum's departure America was seething
with anger at the satire of *Martin Chuzzlewit*, and Dickens's
book was not an isolated attack. *Martin Chuzzlewit* was only the
most recent, if also the most devastating, in a long line of highly
critical books written by British travellers to the United States.
There was a market in Britain for caustic comment on America,

33

as Dickens himself well knew. Seventeen years earlier, in *Pickwick Papers*, he had made Tony Weller suggest that Mr. Pickwick should "have a passage ready taken for 'Merriker'", and then "come back and write a book about the 'Merrikins as'll pay all his expenses and more, if he blows 'em up enough". Between 1820 and 1844 at least one hundred books had been written on America by British travellers, and the consensus of their opinions was overwhelmingly unfavourable.

British travellers to the United States of America in the first half of the nineteenth century found much to criticise: the lack of gaiety; the hurried meals in uncomfortable boarding houses; the slovenliness of the dress; the nasal twang. They also remarked on the absence of culture: the costly and ill-printed books; the universities that better deserved the name of grammar schools; the lack of writers and artists. They doubted if any first-rate minds existed in America, and believed that the smallest English village contained more educated men than any large American town.

The reason for this antipathy was often political. Many of these travellers were Tories, who feared and detested the republican system of the United States. The Tory periodicals—the *Quarterly Review*, *Blackwood's Magazine*, the *Edinburgh Review*—constantly attacked American republicanism, which, they asserted, had made the Americans illiterate, philistine, immoral, irreligious and brutal. According to *Blackwood's Magazine*, America had no education and all the books produced there could be burned without loss. It assured its readers that "there is nothing to awaken fancy in that land of dull reality". Sydney Smith asked, in the *Edinburgh Review*, "who ever read an American book or looked at an American picture?"

The crisis over the Reform Bill in 1832 intensified the Tory attack on American republicanism. Many radicals in Britain were wanting a reformed system of government based on the American model, with its universal franchise. The Tories fought this idea tooth and nail. Those who had been to America wrote of the terrors of republicanism: the mob rule; the election of second-rate men; the corruption in government. They told how the separation of church and state had led to irreligion, on the one hand, and the proliferation of non-conformist sects, on the other. They described the terrible scenes of mass hysteria they had witnessed at the revival meetings, which were a regular feature of so many of these sects.

The Tories found much in America to strengthen their case against republicanism, for their comments, although exaggerated, had much truth in them. Other British travellers, not motivated by political bias, had found the same faults. Those who had travelled beyond the old established Eastern states wrote of the total lack of refinement: the country taverns that expected the guests to sleep two or three in a bed; the unparalleled profanity of the steamboat captains; the inquisitive loafers at every halt; the ubiquitous tobacco chewers spitting jets of brown juice on to pavement or carpet with equal indifference; the duelling in the South; the lawlessness in the South West.

There was also the question of slavery. The British travellers deplored the revolting behaviour of the slave states. They were horrified by the inhumanity of the auctions, which separated husbands from their wives and parents from their children. They despised the hypocrisy of the Northern states, which preached abolition while remaining racially prejudiced. But, above all, they detested the boastfulness, the passion for making money and the love of smart dealing that were the special characteristics of the Yankees, the inhabitants of the New England states.

British travellers in New England were all agreed upon two things: the neatness of the rural scene and the perfidiousness of the inhabitants. They saw in New England a spectacle of industry and prosperity delightful to behold, yet they found the New Englanders themselves to be sly, crafty, deceitful, unscrupulous and dishonest. Mrs. Trollope remarked, "The Yankees (as the New Englanders are called) will avow these qualities themselves with a complacent smile, and boast that no people on earth can match them at over-reaching in a bargain. I have heard them unblushingly relate stories of their cronies and friends, which, if believed among us, would banish the heroes from the fellowship of honest men for ever."

Phineas Taylor Barnum, born in the village of Bethel, Connecticut, on 5 July, 1810, was to be the embodiment of all the Yankee characteristics most detested by the British.

The greatest formative influence on Barnum's early life was his maternal grandfather, after whom he was named Phineas. Old Phineas was admired throughout the district as a very smart man and as an unrivalled master of those two favourite American pastimes, the hoax and the tall story. On the day of his grandson's birth he made over to him the deeds of Ivy Island, a property in a distant corner of the state. For years the boy dreamed of his great inheritance, until, finally, when he was twelve years old he was allowed to journey to Ivy Island and to make the discovery that this was nothing more than five acres of irreclaimable swamp. All the village was in on the joke, and there was great merriment when the boy returned, empty-handed but wiser in the knowledge of the world. He had undergone a form of initiation into manhood similar to that practised by primitive tribes, and known in New England as "cutting the eye-teeth."

Since the birth of his grandson old Phineas had prepared him carefully for this day. During the first six years of the boy's life he gave him pennies to buy sweets, but always instructed him to bargain with the store-keeper to obtain the lowest cash price. Under such training the boy developed precociously the bump of acquisitiveness that is the distinguishing mark of a smart man. He saved his pennies and, at the early age of six, he began business on his own account, selling sweets and gingerbread. He worked hard at his business, and by the time he was nine years old he was self-supporting. He had little regular schooling, but he excelled at arithmetic.

"A correct likeness of the Feejee Mermaid" which appeared
in *The Life of P. T. Barnum*

Idealistic portrayal of mermaids in the New York *Sunday Mercury*

In his early years Barnum came under Methodist influences, and was brought up in fear of hell. There was one meeting-house in the village for all shades of nonconformity, where regular revival meetings were held. These meetings were conducted by itinerant preachers, whose coming was regarded in Puritan Bethel as bright spots in the social calendar. Many of these preachers were fanatics who worked their audience up to a state of hysteria. The emotional excesses of these revival meetings were repugnant to British visitors, especially those who belonged to the established church. Barnum used to return home after these meetings to cry in despair and to beg God to end his existence.

In Bethel Barnum progressed in years, reading his Bible, attending the meeting-house, avoiding bad companions and gaining the respect of the neighbourhood by his genius for smart dealing. At the age of fifteen he broadened his business experience considerably by becoming an assistant in a barter store. None of the items in a barter store had a set price, but were traded for other goods. It would seem that these stores were conducted on the principle of "dog eat dog" or "tit for tat". The customers cheated the storekeeper with their goods and he cheated the customer with his. Cotton was labelled wool, and cotton and wool mixture was labelled silk or linen. Ground coffee was made of burned peas, beans and corn, and ginger was made from corn-meal. "In fact," Barnum says, "everything was different from what it was represented"; a revealing statement in the light of his future enterprises.

A barter store was just the place to stimulate the talents of a youth as smart as Barnum. He swindled all his customers for miles around, to the delight of old Phineas, who agreed, with many others, that the boy was "a chip off the old block". "The tricks of the trade were numerous," Barnum tells us. "If a pedlar wanted to trade with us for a box of beaver hats worth sixty dollars per dozen he was sure to obtain a box of 'coneys' which were dear at fifteen dollars per dozen. If we took our pay in clocks, warranted to keep good time, the chances were that they were no better than a chest of drawers for that purpose . . . and if half the number of wheels necessary to form a clock could be found within the case it was as lucky as extraordinary."

This love of smart dealing was deplored by British visitors. Dickens quoted a dialogue he had held a hundred times in America: " 'Is it not a very disgraceful circumstance that such a man as So and So should be acquiring a large property by the most infamous and odious means, and notwithstanding all the crimes of which he has been guilty, should be tolerated and abetted by your citizens? He is a public nuisance is he not?' 'Yes, sir.' 'A convicted liar?' 'Yes, sir.' 'He has been kicked, and cuffed, and caned?' 'Yes, sir.' 'And he is utterly dishonourable, debased and profligate?' 'Yes, sir.' 'In the name of wonder, then, what is his merit?' 'Well, sir, he is a smart man.' "

This admiration of smart dealing was encountered by British travellers not only in New England but in every state of the Union. The citizens of these other states, however, acknowledged freely, and with no little pride, that smart as they themselves were, the smartest men in the country, or for that matter in the whole world, were to be found in the New England states. This distinction was highly prized by the Yankees, who never neglected an opportunity to brag of exploits that showed their pre-eminence in smart dealing. British visitors were shocked by the stories they heard. "If I were to relate one-tenth part," Mrs. Trollope wrote, "of the dishonest transactions recounted to me by Americans or their fellow-citizens and friends, I am confident that no English reader would give me credit for veracity." She admitted that she had met elsewhere "people who push acuteness to the verge of honesty, and sometimes, perhaps, a little beyond; but, I believe, the Yankee is the only one who will be found to boast of doing so". Thomas Hamilton remarked that the Yankees boasted of transactions so dishonest that they would promptly land an

Englishman in Botany Bay. It was the delight the Americans took in bragging of their smartness that most affronted the British visitor.

In American society fraud had become accepted because everyone practised it. No one could cheat all the people all the time, because they were too busy cheating one another. Fraud permeated American life. It was a competitive country in which there was opportunity for any man to make a lot of money. Each man thought he must get ahead of the other man before the other man got ahead of him. To 'go ahead' was the American axiom. A man must go ahead, no matter how. For this reason, smartness was extolled above honesty, a reversal of values that astounded British visitors.

The position of an assistant in a barter store could not be expected to appeal long to a young man as anxious to go ahead as Barnum. In 1828, at the age of eighteen, he set up to trade "on his own hook" as proprietor of a little store in Bethel. The following summer he married a local tailoress named Charity Hackett, and within a year of their marriage a daughter was born. The responsibility of a wife and family spurred Barnum on to greater efforts. The store did not make money fast enough for his liking, and so, on the advice of old Phineas, he went into the lottery business as well. Lotteries were popular in New England; they were the typical amusement of a people who dearly loved a speculation. Surprisingly enough, considering the Puritan laws of Connecticut, lotteries were not only permitted but were considered a legitimate branch of business. They were even organised for the benefit of churches whose ministers preached against gambling. Old Phineas had made a fortune out of running a lottery, and it appealed to Barnum as a means of getting rich quickly. In the organising of his lottery Barnum showed two of the characteristics that were later to distinguish him as a showman: his flair for doing things on a big scale and his belief in advertising.

He established agents in different towns and sold tickets all over the state. He distributed hand bills. He inserted advertisements in newspapers.

No matter how busy he was, Barnum, like his grandfather, would always take time off to indulge in a hoax or to tell a tall story. The point of both the hoax and the tall story was to come off best, no matter how many lies needed to be told. As both depended on fraud, they were favourite American pastimes. The greatest of Barnum's humbugs as a showman were extensions of the hoaxes he hatched and the tall stories he told in the company of his cronies, who gathered in his store at Bethel.

The tall story had been popular in America since Colonial days: it satisfied a deep need in the American character. In such a vast country a man often felt lonely and uncertain, even in the settled Eastern states. At times he seemed to be living on the edge of an outlandish and hostile continent. He needed to be reassured by a human voice, either his own or someone else's, talking on and on to dispel his melancholy. And nothing was more reassuring to hear than the tall story, in which the hero always came out on top, confident of the future.

For Americans were convinced that the future belonged to them. They were an energetic people in a land of opportunity. Britain and the old sophisticated nations of Europe might condescend towards them, but the Americans were certain that time would tell. Europe was effete; America vigorous. By 1835 six hundred thousand square miles of her territory had been settled, and the frontier was moving westward at the average rate of seventeen miles a year. Farms were established on virgin lands that had never known a plough. Steamboats and railways were cutting deep into the wilderness. Industrial towns were being built on sites that had known no other habitations than the lodges of Indian tribes.

Such great events brought forth great heroes, whose exploits were enshrined in the tall story. Men who could fight harder and shoot straighter, eat more and drink deeper than any other mortal. Stories were told of the number of Indians they had shot, the height of the mountains they had climbed, the length of the rivers they had sailed. An audience gathered quickly round the man who could tell of these heroes of the new American mythology, supermen in the land of endless opportunity.

Their need for the human voice made Americans ready audiences for politicians, clergymen, pedlars and showmen. Political oratory, with its extravagance of language and promises, was especially popular, because of its natural affinities with the tall story. Political meetings, like revival meetings, were highly regarded social events. They were not confined to questions of great moment, but were held at the drop of a hat to air the most trivial issues. They were the perfect occasion for the human voice to be heard at length. This obsession with politics puzzled British visitors. They were astonished to hear heated arguments over elections that were not due to take place for three years. Discussing politics and reading newspapers were the two most popular recreations in America. The two interests were inseparable, because politics at federal, state and parish level were fully reported in the newspapers, and a regular perusal was essential if one were not to be left out of the never-ending discussions.

Barnum, like all Americans, loved to air his political opinions, not only in discussion but also in print; and there was at that time a burning issue in New England on which he wanted his views to be known to a larger audience than that which frequented his store. Religious fanaticism had always flourished in New England, and in 1831 certain ministers were calling for a Christian party in politics. To Barnum this appeared to be an encroachment on the First Amendment to the Constitution of the United States of America, the Separation of Church and State. He wrote several letters and articles to the local paper to arouse the public to an awareness of the danger, but these were not printed. Barnum regarded this as nothing less than the silencing of free opinion, and to show he was a man to be reckoned with he started his own weekly newspaper, *The Herald of Freedom*, which "would oppose all combinations against the liberty of our country". He tells us that "the boldness and vigor with which the paper was conducted soon commanded a liberal circulation, not only in the vicinity of its publication, but large numbers were sent into nearly every state in the Union".

When the first issue of *The Herald of Freedom* appeared on 19 October, 1831, Barnum was barely twenty-one years old and had never voted. So it would seem that Dickens did not exaggerate when he created, in *Martin Chuzzlewit*, the character of Jefferson Brick, boy War Correspondent of the "New York Rowdy Journal", who believed his articles were anxiously read by the British Parliament and the Court of St. James's "and had a mighty influence upon the cabinets of Eu-rope". We do not know whether Barnum, like Brick, believed that his articles "struck the deadliest blow at the hundred heads of the Hydra of Corruption, now grovelling in the dust beneath the lance of Reason"; and that "the libation of freedom" must sometimes be quaffed in blood. But we do know that whatever the issue, at whatever the cost, Barnum, like the boy wonder of the "New York Rowdy Journal", was always to be found "at his usual post in the van of human civilisation and moral purity", for Barnum himself assures us that this was so.

"Impelled by the vehemence of youth," he tells us, "and without the caution of experience or the dread of consequences, I repeatedly laid myself open to legal difficulty under the law of libel, and three times during my career as editor, I was prosecuted." On one of these occasions he was sentenced to sixty days in jail. *The Herald of Freedom* had accused a local deacon of being "guilty of taking usury of an orphan boy". A deacon was a powerful person in Connecticut. Under the strict Puritan laws of the state, he had the authority to arrest anyone found riding on horseback or in a carriage between sundown on Saturday and sundown on

Sunday. This particular deacon was a grocer, and had Barnum accused him of extortion, he would probably never have brought the case to court. But usury was a different matter. This was an ungodly practice, expressly forbidden in the Bible. The court took a serious view, and Barnum was sentenced to sixty days in jail and a fine of one hundred dollars.

The whole affair turned out to be a triumph for Barnum. To many of his fellow-citizens he was a hero, for there was a general feeling that his imprisonment infringed upon two great articles of the Constitution: Separation of Church and State and Freedom of the Press. Barnum enjoyed his popularity. His imprisonment was not a hardship. He was comfortably lodged at Danbury jail, three miles from Bethel. He had had his cell papered and carpeted before taking possession. He received a constant flow of visitors and continued to edit his newspaper, which, because of his martyrdom, now had an increased circulation.

Not in all the burlesque of *Martin Chuzzlewit* is there a scene to match the one that followed Barnum's release from jail. He was the guest of honour at a banquet, during which an ode and an oration on the Freedom of the Press were delivered, and toasts and speeches celebrated his courageous stand for liberty. Then came the most imposing part of the ceremony. Barnum and a brass band took their seats in an open coach drawn by six horses. The coach, which had been especially decorated for the occasion, was preceded by forty horsemen, and a marshal bearing the flag of the United States. Behind the coach came the carriage of the Orator and the President of the Day, followed by the Committee of Arrangements and sixty carriages of citizens. A salvo of cannon marked the commencement of the march, and the procession set off to the cheers of hundreds of people who lined the road. The band played a selection of national airs, in which 'Yankee Doodle' featured several times, until their arrival in Bethel, where they struck up the tune of 'Home Sweet Home'. So Barnum was borne in triumph from Danbury to Bethel.

It was inevitable that such a man could not be content to remain long as a storekeeper in an obscure village in Connecticut. Barnum knew he was not in his natural sphere and that he was meant for bigger things. 1834 was a year of decision. The state of Connecticut had lately passed a law forbidding lotteries, which deprived him of his main source of income. He still had his store, but he found mercantile life too laborious and its returns too slow. He still had *The Herald of Freedom*, which he enjoyed editing. He wrote most of the newspaper himself, and it provided a satisfactory vehicle for the opinions that he was always ready to give on political, economic, religious and social topics. But *The Herald of Freedom* did not make money and, above all else, Barnum wanted to make money. He wanted to make a lot of money, he wanted to make it easily, he wanted to make it quickly. In other words, he wanted to "go ahead". And he was very much aware that he was already twenty-four years old, an age by which many a citizen of this young and progressive country had either made his pile of dollars or was well on the way to doing so. Barnum decided that he must lose no more time. He sold his store, gave over the management of *The Herald of Freedom* to his brother-in-law and, towards the end of 1834, he brought his wife and family to New York, where he hoped to make his fortune.

In 1834 New York was a bustling metropolis with a population of over two hundred thousand. Even British visitors, who found so much to criticise in America, agreed that New York was a fine city, although the enthusiasm with which they described its beauties owed much to the fact that this was their first landfall after being confined for three weeks in a storm-tossed packet boat. They leaped ashore prepared to admire anything, so thankful were they to find themselves again on solid ground. Mrs. Trollope described New York as "a lovely and noble city" rising "like Venice from the sea". She admired the handsome houses of the rich in Hudson Square—"the equal of any square in London"—

with its fine gravelled walks enclosed by an iron railing "as high and as handsome as that of the Tuileries". She was enchanted by Broadway, with its fine shops and elegant carriages, perhaps not the equal of Bond Street and Regent Street, but magnificent in its extent.

Dickens, too, wrote enthusiastically of New York. There were, of course, side streets "as clean or as dirty" as side streets in London. There were also, as in London, the dreary working-class districts, such as the Bowery, dominated by the famous prison The Tombs, with its bastard Egyptian architecture, and the notorious Five Points, "as filthy and wretched as St. Giles's". But he loved the fine streets and squares and the spacious houses.

At first many things in New York reminded the British visitors of the mother country. The signs over the shops were written in English; the language spoken, though different in tone, was also English. Yet there was a foreignness about everything. Basil Hall wrote, "The whole seemed at times more like a dream than a sober reality. For there was so much about it that looked like England that we half fancied ourselves back again; and yet there was quite enough to show in the next instant that it was a very different country." As the alien nature of America became more and more apparent, the British visitors grew uneasy, until, by the end of their stay, their attitude had generally become one of downright hostility. This attitude was reflected in the majority of books on America written by British travellers.

These books had a depressing effect upon the Americans. As citizens of a young nation, they were sensitive to all foreign criticism, but the opinions of the British were the only ones that counted for anything with them. The others they could dismiss if they chose, but they could not ignore British criticism. Although the Americans had broken away from Britain, they were still culturally dependent upon her. The books they read were British books. The models for every author, artist or lawyer were British. America wanted the admiration of Britain above that of all other countries, for they still regarded her as their legitimate, if somewhat stony-hearted, mother. "Well, how's the unnat'ral old parent by this time?" an American asks Martin Chuzzlewit. "Progressing back'ards, I expect, as usual?"

The Americans were vulnerable to British criticism, and these books wounded their national pride. They could not understand why the authors wrote at length about their faults, yet said little about their great achievement in carving a nation out of a vast continent in so short a span of years. This omission was partly the fault of the Americans themselves. They could not talk about their country without boasting. This craving for admiration affronted the British visitors, with the result that they often refused even to give the Americans the praise they deserved. American brag was only the sign of a young country uncertain of its position in the world, but only a few British visitors made any allowance for this. Some of them saw America as an awkward, adolescent nation and wrote with sympathy and understanding of its problems. But most British travellers did not have this perception. They did not see America as a new and emerging nation. They still regarded the country as a British province. The Americans, therefore, as a provincial people, were hardly to be taken seriously. This view of America was widely held in Britain. When Dickens announced that he was going to America to write a book about the Americans some of his friends thought he was making a long journey to little purpose. "Why can't you go down to Bristol," Lady Holland asked him, "and see some of the third- and fourth-class people there and they'll do just as well?"

This condescending attitude had a cumulative effect on Americans, resulting in a morbid sensitivity to British criticism. The American reaction to *Travels in North America*, by Captain Basil Hall, published in 1829, was an early manifestation of this excessive touchiness. No other book by a British traveller had exasperated the Americans so much, yet the book was fairer and less critical than many previous ones. As a Tory, Captain Hall did not believe that the British had anything to learn from the American system of government. He wrote this as the crisis that led to the Reform Bill was looming up. His Tory patriotism made him condemn all American political institutions, for he could not bear the thought of any change in Britain. His attempt to analyse American society was also unsympathetic, but, whenever his prejudices allowed, he praised frequently and with pleasure.

Hall's *Travels in North America*, restrained as it was, outraged the Americans. The book seemed to touch an exposed nerve. Mrs. Frances Trollope, who was living in America at the time, described its reception as "a sort of moral earthquake", and the vibrations were still being felt when she left the country two years later. "Other nations have been called thin-skinned," she commented, "but the citizens of the Union have, apparently, no skins at all; they wince if a breeze blows over them, unless it be tempered with adulation." The Rowdy Press declared, with much vituperation, that the book contained not a word of truth from beginning to end. One newspaper speculated on the motives that had caused Captain Hall to visit America, and suggested that he had been sent out by the Tories with the express purpose of checking the growing admiration of the British people for the government of the United States. An anonymous work was published in New York, which stated that Captain Hall had not only slandered the Americans but was himself a man of questionable character and low morals. The fact that the gallant Captain had gone out of his way to record every small act of kindness was even held against him. All Americans agreed that to bear testimony to the unvarying kindness of his reception, on the one hand, and yet find fault with the country, on the other, was nothing less than the most abominable ingratitude.

The Americans were to be even more furious when Mrs. Trollope's own account of her experiences in America was published three years later. Mrs. Trollope had lived in Cincinnati between 1827 and 1831. Back in Britain, she wrote *Domestic*

Manners of the Americans. This was published in 1832, the year of the Reform Bill. A traveller in America, the following year, found the controversy over her book had eclipsed all other interests. "At every corner of the street," he reported, "at the door of every petty retailer of information for the people, a large placard met the eye, with 'For sale here, with plates, *Domestic Manners of the Americans* by Mrs. Trollope.' At every table d'hôte, on board of every steamboat, and in all societies, the first question was, 'Have you read Mrs. Trollope?' And one-half of the people would be seen with a red or blue half-bound volume in their hand, which you might vouch for being the odious work, and the more it was abused, the more rapidly did the printers issue new editions."

Domestic Manners of the Americans was the most anti-American book that had yet been written by a British visitor to the United States. As thorough a Tory as Captain Hall, Mrs. Trollope detested the American form of government. She deplored the constant boasting by Americans of their 'unequalled freedom" and their "glorious institutions", and declared that she could not understand the phrases. "Yet still I was in the dark," she wrote, "nor can I guess what they mean, unless they call incessant electioneering, without pause or interval, for a single day, for a single hour, of their whole existence 'a glorious institution'. Their unequalled freedom, I think, I understand better. Their code of common law is built upon ours; and the difference between us is this, in England the laws are acted upon, in America they are not."

Such tart comments on American republicanism were only to be expected from an anti-Reform Tory. It was in her descriptions of the social life of America that Mrs. Trollope gave most offence. Here her remarks showed a dislike that bordered on malevolence. She said of Americans, "I do not like their principles, I do not like their manners, I do not like their opinions." In all her travels, she never saw "an American man walk or stand well". Her "honest conviction" after four years of "attentive and earnest observation and enquiry" was "that the standard of moral character in the United States is greatly lower than in Europe".

Mrs. Trollope believed that all Americans were philistines, with little feeling for art and literature. "Perhaps they are right," she observed. "In Europe we see fortunes crippled by a passion for statues, or for pictures, or for books, or for gems; for all and every of the artificial wants that give grace to life, and tend to make man forget that he is a thing of clay. They are wiser in their generation on the other side of the Atlantic; I rarely saw anything that led to such oblivion there." The best literary conversation she held was with a gentleman in Cincinnati who had never heard of Massinger and Ford; who dismissed Chaucer and Spenser by saying he thought it affected to talk of authors who wrote in a tongue no longer intelligible; who thought Byron immoral, Shakespeare obscene and the title of Pope's 'Rape of the Lock' sufficient to debar any decent person from reading it.

Wherever she went in America, she found the atmosphere dreary and utilitarian. "I never saw a population so totally divested of gaiety," she wrote; "there is no trace of this feeling from one end of the Union to another. They have no fêtes, no fairs, no merrymakings, no music in the streets, no Punch, no puppet shows." Cincinnati was a "triste little town", with no concerts or dinner parties; billiards and cards forbidden by law; and revival meetings the chief social attraction. "How often," she wrote, "did our homely adage occur to me, 'All work and no play would make Jack a dull boy'; Jonathan is a very dull boy. We are by no means so gay as our lively neighbours on the other side of the Channel, but compared with Americans, we are whirligigs and tetotums; every day is a holyday and every night a festival."

However much the Americans disagreed with Mrs. Trollope, there were some, Barnum among them, who shared her views on the drabness of American life. Barnum recognised that it was the duty of everyone to work and make money, but he also believed that people needed to be amused in their leisure hours. As a show-man, he was to dissipate the universal gloom that stifled America, but when he first arrived in New York he had no idea how he would make his living. He had no particular career in mind, but, as a start, he wanted a job where he would receive a portion of the profits. He had no intention of working for a fixed salary. Such a position was not easy to find, for he soon discovered that most of the men in New York were looking for the same kind of situation. Every morning he scanned the "Wants" column in the *New York Sun*, which was crowded with temptingly worded propositions such as "Immense speculation on a small capital", "$1000 dollars easily made in one year", and "Twenty dollars a day could be earned without any capital".

"Fortunes equalling that of Croesus, and as plenty as black-berries," Barnum wrote, "were dangling from many an adver-tisement which mysteriously invited the reader to apply at Room No. 16, in the fifth storey of a house in some retired and uninviting locality; but when I had wended my way up flights of dark, rickety, greasy stairs, and through sombre, narrow passages I would find that my fortune depended firstly upon my advancing a certain sum of money, from three dollars to five hundred as the case might be; and secondly, upon my success in peddling a newly-discovered patent life-pill, an ingenious mousetrap, or something of the sort." And no matter how quickly he set off to answer an advertisement, he found, more often than not, at least twenty others there before him, and as they departed disappointed, new applicants continued to arrive.

New York was filled with go-ahead young men, all with the same aim as Barnum—to make money quickly. This universal pursuit of money was an American characteristic frequently commented on by British visitors. Mrs. Trollope tells of an Englishman, long resident in America, who declared "that in following, in meeting, or in overtaking, in the street, on the road, or in the field, at the theatre, the coffee-house, or at home, he had never overheard Americans conversing without the word DOLLAR being pronounced between them". Dickens remarked that the greater part of American conversation could be summed up in one word. *Dollars.* "All their cares, hopes, joys, affections, virtues and associations," he wrote, "seemed to be melted down into dollars. Whatever the chance contributions that fell into the slow cauldron of their talk, they made the gruel thick and slab with dollars. Men were weighed by their dollars, measures gauged by their dollars; life was auctioneered, appraised, put up, and knocked down for its dollars."

This pervading air of business, so serious and so melancholy, oppressed the British visitor. "We are a trading nation" was the reason given by the Americans for all social deficiencies and uncomfortable habits such as married people living in boarding houses and seldom meeting from early morning until late at night except at public meals. These meals were eaten silently and quickly. Captain Basil Hall found that in such company all his attempts to start a conversation proved abortive, "for each person seemed intent exclusively on the professed business of the meeting, and having dispatched, in all haste, what sustenance was required, and in solemn silence, rose and departed. It might have been thought we had assembled rather for the purpose of inhuming the body of some departed friend than of merrily keeping alive the existing generation." The sole object of eating was to get through a necessary amount of food as quickly as possible, and during the meal they were haunted by the thought of what their competitors were up to while they sat at table. "Great heaps of indigestible matter melted away as ice before the sun," Dickens observed. "It was a solemn and an awful thing to see. Dyspeptic individuals bolted their food in wedges; feeding, not themselves, but broods of nightmares, who were continually standing at livery within them. Spare men, with lank and rigid cheeks, came out unsatisfied from the destruction of heavy dishes, and glared with watchful eyes upon the pastry."

In such frenetic company Barnum did not, at first, distinguish himself. All his running at the beck of advertisements availed him nothing. During the entire winter he could not find a situation. In the spring he opened a boarding house and bought an interest in a grocery store. Neither of these was a promising prospect, but he was optimistic. He regarded his position as no more than a temporary arrangement, and he was continually on the look-out for something better to turn up. Nor had he long to wait. In July a friend, Coley Bartram, of Reading, Connecticut, called on him and gave him some interesting news about the old Negress Joice Heth, who claimed to be one hundred and sixty-one years old and to have been the nurse of George Washington, the father of the United States of America.

Chapter Three

THE CHAMPION OF THE 'MERRIKINS

WITH JOICE HETH, Barnum began his career as a showman. In the promotion of this sanctimonious old hypocrite, he demonstrated, for the first time, that appreciation of publicity, that belief in the power of the Press and that genius for turning every event to his own advantage which were to characterise all his enterprises. But his early ventures in showmanship were not always successful. Signor Vivalla, his second exhibit, did not have the drawing power of Joice Heth. The little Italian had not the religious appeal that had made Joice so popular, and he could hardly be expected to round off his performance, as she had done, with a session of hymn singing. Barnum did all he could to arouse the curiosity of the public in his juggler by playing first on their preference for foreign entertainers and then on their patriotism by matching him against an American, but despite all his efforts, interest in Vivalla soon faded.

The year 1836 was a bad one for Barnum. Joice Heth died on 19 February, leaving him with Signor Vivalla as his only asset, and the juggler was not bringing in much money. In April, nothing better turning up, Barnum and Vivalla joined forces with a small travelling circus. During the summer they toured New Jersey, Pennsylvania, Delaware, Maryland and North Carolina. Barnum did not enjoy travelling. He hated to be away from his wife and family. But he decided that if he must travel he would at least travel with his own show. In October he bought four horses and two waggons, and hired Vivalla, a nigger minstrel and a clown

E   53

to form a show, which travelled under the grandiloquent title of 'Barnum's Grand Scientific and Musical Theatre'.

Barnum took his show on a tour of the South West, through the frontier states, where any kind of entertainment was sure of a welcome. But life in these places was filled with dangers and privations. Outside the Eastern states there was little regard for the law. British travellers gave lurid descriptions of the South West. They wrote of the fights with knives and guns; the gambling and drunkenness; the frequent lynchings. Barnum found that such people made uncouth and dangerous audiences. But as he could not find an exhibit worthy of New York, he was forced to make two tours of the South West during the next two years. In June, 1838, he returned to New York, weary and disillusioned. He disbanded the show, sold the effects and vowed never again to be a travelling showman.

Barnum found himself again looking through the "Wants" advertisements in the New York papers. The sale of "Barnum's Grand Scientific and Musical Theatre" had given him a little capital, and he advertised to become a partner in a respectable business, stating that he had $2500, in cash, to invest. He received ninety-three replies from brokers, lottery promoters, inventors, patent-medicine men and from others who declined to name their business, but promised, if he granted them a confidential interview, to put him on the road to untold wealth. He finally chose to enter into partnership with a German named Proler, who was the manufacturer of "Proler's Genuine Bear Grease", advertised to "cover a bald head with beautiful, glossy, curly hair as quickly as any other composition yet discovered". Proler did not rely solely on the irrefutable truth of this advertisement to sell his product. To increase even more the faith of his customers, he exhibited a live bear in front of his store, with the label "To be slaughtered next". Altogether, he seemed to Barnum to conduct his business along the right lines. Indeed, when Barnum worked with Proler he realised he was in the presence of a master of advertising. But he was not in that presence for long. Shortly afterwards the German swindled him out of his money and sailed for Rotterdam, leaving him the secret recipe of the Genuine Bear's Grease, a compound of pigs' lard, mutton tallow and oil of lavender.

So, in the spring of 1840, Barnum was forced to take up again the life of a travelling showman. He got together a comedian, a Negro dancer and a fiddler, and "Barnum's Grand Scientific and Musical Theatre" set off for a tour of the South and the South West. By the time they reached New Orleans the comedian had deserted. At Mobile the Negro dancer absconded with some of Barnum's money. There was little point in continuing the tour, and Barnum and his faithful fiddler made their way homewards by the Mississippi and the Ohio.

This was the lowest point in Barnum's career. Despite all his efforts, he could not find a congenial position. Living in New York, with nothing to do and a family to support, soon exhausted his funds, and he tells us that he became "about as poor as I should ever wish to be". He was thirty-one years old, an age by which he should have made his fortune. While men were out-smarting one another on all sides and adding daily to their piles of dollars, he remained a failure. He dreamed of a great business opportunity that would provide not only for the present but also for the future.

This was Barnum's position when, towards the end of 1841, he learned that Scudder's American Museum was for sale. It was at the corner of Broadway and Ann Street, and not the scientific institution its name might suggest. It was mainly a collection of curiosities brought home by sea captains from the East. The most interesting specimens were stuffed animals, a live anaconda and a tame alligator. There was also a gallery of dubious paintings, supposed to be national portraits. Barnum believed the Museum was the opportunity he had been waiting for, and he was prepared to go to any lengths to buy it. The Museum had been losing money for some years and the asking price was low. But it was more than Barnum could afford. "*You* buy the American Museum?" said an astonished friend; "What do you intend buying it with?" "*Brass,*" Barnum replied, "for silver and gold I have none."

And it was sheer effrontery that gained Barnum control of the American Museum. The way in which he conducted the negotiations was astounding even by Yankee standards. He ruined public confidence in a company who were offering a better price for the Museum by getting his friends in the Rowdy Press to print false information about the company's affairs. He clinched the deal by using as security his worthless inheritance of Ivy Island. On 1 January, 1842, he took over the American Museum. Barnum had arrived on Broadway.

Not even London had a thoroughfare to equal Broadway, four miles long, running the extent of the city and ending in open country. Dickens, who visited America in 1842, was fascinated by it. He was amazed at the number of omnibuses—"half-a-dozen have gone by in as many minutes!"—the press of hackney cabs, gigs and phaëtons, and the pigs, the city scavengers, roaming about in scores. He admired the glittering shops, the pineapples and watermelons profusely displayed, the great glittering blocks of ice being carried into bar-rooms. And the people. The elegant ladies—"what various parasols! what rainbow silks and satins!"—the clerks and shop assistants with their cultivated whiskers—"Byrons of the desk and counter"—the Irish labourers in holiday clothes, Dutch farmers from Pennsylvania, Quakers, freed Negroes and the immigrants, straight off the boats, still clutching their bundles. Everybody came to Broadway to join in the great parade.

Within less than a year Barnum had made the American Museum the greatest place of entertainment in America. He transformed the drab exterior of the building by mounting on the walls large oval paintings of exotic birds, beasts and reptiles.

Banners with the inscription BARNUM'S AMERICAN MUSEUM streamed out over the roof. On the first floor balcony a brass band played "Free Music for the Million" above the jostling crowds on Broadway. By night the Museum was illuminated by the first floodlights ever seen in New York. "I thoroughly understood the art of advertising," Barnum wrote, "not merely by means of printer's ink, which I have always used freely, and to which I confess myself so much indebted for my success, but by turning every possible circumstance to my account. It was my monomania to make the Museum the town wonder and town talk."

Under his magic touch an Indian war club became "The Club that Killed Captain Cook". The roof of the Museum, with the addition of a few pots of flowers, became "The Aerial Garden". His gift of language made his wonders even more wonderful. A hippopotamus was advertised as "The Great Behemoth of the Scriptures". His performing fleas were "harnessed to carriages and other vehicles of several times their own weight, which they will draw with as much precision as a cart-horse". His Museum contained "a million of things in every branch of Nature and Art, comprehending a Cyclopaedical Synopsis of everything worth seeing and knowing in this curious world's curious economy".

He gave his patrons a superfluity of novelties, not from generosity but because he believed that to send them away more than satisfied made them come again and bring their friends. "I meant to make people talk about my Museum," he wrote; "to exclaim over its wonders; to have men and women all over the country say: 'There is no place in the United States where so much can be seen for twenty-five cents as in Barnum's American Museum.'" Because he believed his exhibits to be worth three times the price of admission, he was not scrupulous about the methods he used to advertise them. His aim was to make people think, talk and wonder about his Museum and, as a result, pay it a visit. He wrote, "It was the world's way then as it is now, to excite the community with flaming posters, promising almost everything for next to nothing. I confess that I took no pains to set my enterprising fellow-citizens a better example. I fell in with the world's way; and if my 'puffing' was more persistent, my advertising more audacious, my posters more glaring, my pictures more exaggerated, my flags more patriotic and my transparencies more brilliant than they would have been under the management of my neighbours, it was not because I had less scruple than they, but more energy, far more ingenuity, and a better foundation for such promises."

Throughout 1842 Barnum diversified the attractions at the Museum with "whatever money could buy and enterprise secure". At various times he exhibited a rhinoceros, grizzly bears, orang-outangs, great serpents, educated dogs, jugglers, gipsies, albinos, fat boys, giants, dwarfs, rope dancers, Red Indians and the Feejee Mermaid. He was constantly on the lookout for new attractions from Europe, Africa and the Far East, but, ironically, towards the end of the year, in the gloomy Puritanical state of Connecticut, the last place he expected to find wonders and marvels of any kind, he discovered the greatest exhibit he was ever to have in his entire career as a showman.

In November, 1842, he was in Albany on business and, as the Hudson River was frozen over and no boats sailing, he returned to New York by the Housatonic Railroad, stopping one night at Bridgeport, Connecticut, with his half-brother, Philo, who kept the Franklin Hotel. Bridgeport was a small community of whale fishers and farmers situated on the north shore of Long Island Sound. Barnum remembered that he had once heard of "a remarkably small child" who lived there. He asked Philo if he knew of such a child. Philo told him that he must be referring to the son of Sherwood Stratton, the carpenter. Barnum asked his brother to arrange a meeting, and the next morning the child and his parents came to the hotel.

When Barnum saw the child he was astonished. The boy was so tiny that he barely came up to the showman's knee. He was a perfectly formed, bright-eyed little fellow with fair hair and rosy cheeks, but he was only twenty-five inches in height. His name was Charles Sherwood Stratton and he was four years old.

His parents told Barnum that at birth there had been nothing to indicate that their child would be anything but normal. At six months he weighed fifteen pounds two ounces, but he was still this weight at twelve months and had not grown an inch. When he remained the same height and weight year after year they realised they had a dwarf in the family. Strictly speaking, Charles S. Stratton was not a dwarf but a midget. A dwarf has a normal upper body, but his lower limbs are misshapen, because of a defective thyroid. In appearance he is grotesque and often repulsive. A midget, on the other hand, is perfectly proportioned, a human being on a smaller scale. His stunted growth is the result of a defective pituitary gland. These distinctions were unknown to medical science until 1886, three years after Charles Stratton's death, so during his lifetime he was always referred to as a dwarf.

Unaware of the reasons for stunted growth, the Strattons had, at first, regarded Charles as a mark of God's disfavour. Their other children were normal and there was nothing in the history of either family to explain this misfortune. But, as the child grew older, they saw no reason to hide him away. There was nothing deformed or repulsive about him; indeed, he was delightful to look upon. He played naturally with other children. Everyone in Bridgeport had grown used to him; they no longer considered him either abnormal or curious.

When Barnum asked the Strattons to allow him to exhibit their son at the American Museum they agreed. They were poor people, and the money would be useful to them. Moreover, Barnum had assured them that their son would be exhibited not as a freak but as the charming little fellow he was. Barnum was very cautious over the chances of success. He had no reason to doubt the facts about Charles that the Strattons had given him, but, after all, the child was only four years old, and all chances of growing had not passed. To exhibit a dwarf of that age might provoke the question, How do you know he is a dwarf? Barnum wrote, "Some license might be taken with the facts, but even with this advantage I really felt that the adventure was nothing more than an experiment, and I engaged him for the short term of four weeks at three dollars per week—all charges, including travelling and boarding of himself and mother, being at my expense."

When Mrs. Stratton brought her little boy to New York, on 8 December, 1842, she was astonished to see posters and billboards everywhere proclaiming,

P. T. Barnum of the American Museum, Broadway at Ann Street, is proud to announce that he has imported from London to add to his collection of extraordinary curiosities from all over the world, the rarest, the tiniest, the most diminutive dwarf imaginable—TOM THUMB, ELEVEN YEARS OLD AND ONLY TWENTY-FIVE INCHES HIGH, JUST ARRIVED FROM ENGLAND!!!

Barnum had given young Charles British nationality because, as with Signor Vivalla, the juggler, he wanted to take advantage of his countrymen's preference for foreign exhibits. He had more than doubled the child's age because he believed that had he announced him as being only four years old it would have been impossible to arouse the curiosity of the public. Calling the child after Sir Tom Thumb, the inch-long knight of King Arthur's Court, was a stroke of genius. No dwarf ever had a better name.

Before exhibiting Tom Thumb at the American Museum, Barnum coached him in comic routines, patter and songs. "I took great pains to train my diminutive prodigy," he wrote, "devoting many hours to that purpose, by day and by night, and succeeded, because he had native talent and an intense love of the ludicrous.

He became very fond of me." Barnum also fitted him out with a wardrobe of clothes specially tailored to his size. Dressed in one of his new outfits, the dwarf was taken by Barnum on a round of visits to newspaper editors. They stared in amazement at this dandified little creature dressed in a grey beaver hat, grey suit, flowered satin vest, frilled shirt and high stiff stock. Tom Thumb stood before them, leaning on his silver topped cane with all the nonchalance of a man-about-town. One editor was having dinner with his family when Barnum and Tom Thumb arrived. The dwarf was lifted on to the table, where he picked his way among the cutlery and supervised the carving of the turkey, while the children shrieked with delight and warned him not to fall into a wine glass and drown himself. The newspapers published such enthusiastic accounts of Tom Thumb that their readers were anxious to see for themselves this wonderful little man from England.

When Tom Thumb made his début at the American Museum the lecture room was crowded. After Barnum had introduced him to the audience the dwarf began his performance with a monologue that bristled with puns. "Good evening, ladies and gentleman," he said, in a Cockney accent, "I am only a Thumb, but a good hand in a general way at amusing you, for though a mite I am mighty . . ." Barnum had noticed that one formed a better idea of the dwarf's smallness when he was contrasted with another child, so he next invited a little boy to step on to the platform. "I'd rather have a little miss," said Tom Thumb pertly, thus gaining, from the outset, the great reputation as a ladies man that he was to enjoy throughout his career.

In the second part of his programme he appeared as a soldier of the American Revolution, dressed in white wig, black cocked hat, blue coat, white waistcoat and breeches, with a ten-inch-long sword in his hand. He went through the paces of a military drill, while singing "Yankee Doodle". Throughout the month he was to appear in a variety of roles. As Napoleon in exile at St. Helena, he paced the stage in sombre meditation. As David he fought against Goliath, played by one of the Museum's giants. As a sailor, he danced the hornpipe and sang "A Life on the Ocean Wave".

Tom Thumb became the talk of the town, and at the end of the four weeks Barnum re-engaged him for a year at an increased salary of seven dollars a week, with the right to exhibit him in any part of the United States. Any fears the Strattons might have had about their child becoming a performer had now been overcome. The boy was obviously happy in his work, and the money he was earning was more than welcome to them. Moreover, they were pleased that Barnum was taking steps to ensure that their son would enjoy some measure of normal life in his new career. They were to accompany him on all his tours, the father acting as ticket seller. A tutor was employed and time set aside each day for study and play.

During 1843 Tom Thumb visited all the major cities and towns in the United States. In many places the fame of the dwarf had gone before him. The New York correspondent of the *Baltimore Sun* wrote, "I cannot describe the sensations with which one looks upon the diminutive specimen of humanity. Were he deformed, or sickly, or melancholy, we might pity him; but he is so manly, so handsome, so hearty, and so happy, that we look upon him as a being from another sphere. General Tom Thumb, as you may well imagine, attracted crowds; indeed, not less than thirty thousand persons visited him at the American Museum. Gentlemen of the finest distinction invited him to dine at their houses; charming ladies came in their carriages, and made him valuable presents, and he was for six weeks *the lion*. I understand that he is meeting with a similar reception in Philadelphia; and as he will probably visit the Monumental City before he returns, you will have an opportunity of seeing him and verifying my description." These tours were so successful that Barnum voluntarily increased Tom Thumb's salary to twenty-five dollars a week. He even dropped the pretence of calling the dwarf English, for he found that audiences were more pleased to learn that this wonderful little creature belonged to America. But he never deducted the six extra years he had added to the dwarf's age.

In January, 1844, Barnum engaged Tom Thumb for another year at fifty dollars a week and all expenses, with the right to exhibit him in Europe. The success of the past year had convinced him that in Tom Thumb he had one of the greatest attractions in the world. He believed that if he were to exploit the dwarf to the full he must seek a wider field of operation than America. He booked passages for himself, Tom Thumb, the dwarf's parents and his tutor on the *Yorkshire*, which was scheduled to sail from New York to Liverpool on 16 January, 1844.

An American could not have chosen a worse time to visit Britain. Relations between the two countries were at their lowest ebb since the American Revolution. All the condescension, mockery and contempt that the British had for America had culminated in the most devastating attack ever inflicted on that country by a British writer. Charles Dickens had recently published the American chapters of *Martin Chuzzlewit*, and while the British roared with laughter, the Americans howled with rage.

When Dickens had first visited America, two years earlier, he had come in the friendliest spirit, ready to admire everything. He was sympathetic to the United States as a democratic, kingless country, free from class rule. He believed America to be a more humane and more enlightened country than Britain, with much to offer "the unnat'ral old parent". He was convinced that he, as a Radical, could understand the country in a way that the Tories could not. He decided to visit America and write a book that would redress their unfavourable opinions. This was not his only reason. There was in Britain an established market for books on America, and he hoped his book would do well.

Dickens was as popular in America as he was in Britain, and when he arrived there, in 1842, he was given a triumphant reception. Never since Lafayette had a foreigner been given such a welcome. No British visitor had ever come to America better disposed than Dickens, but the more he saw of the country, the more uneasy he became. There was not the abolition of poverty he had expected to find; the running of schools, prisons and workhouses was no more enlightened than in Britain; and he found in the corruption of politicians, the rowdiness of the Press and the horrors of slavery, evils he had never before encountered. "This is not the republic I came to see," he wrote to Macready, "this is not the republic of my imagination."

American Notes, by Charles Dickens, was published in 1842. Almost as soon as it appeared in the British bookshops, pirated editions flooded the United States. In *American Notes* Dickens found much to praise in America, especially the fineness of the towns, but his admiration was outweighed by his abhorrence of the dreary social life, the philistinism and the universal love of smart dealing. The book was received by the American Press with derision. Bennett wrote in the *New York Herald* that Dickens had "the most coarse, vulgar, impudent and superficial mind" ever to write about "this original and remarkable country". Yet *American Notes* was a mild enough book compared to Mrs. Trollope's *Domestic Manners of the Americans*.

But it is not hard to understand the bitter reaction of the Americans to Dickens's book. From him they had expected so much more. For years British travellers had come to America and then returned to their own country to write the almost statutory anti-American account of their experiences. The Americans were certain that in Charles Dickens they had, at last, the man who would give a true and favourable picture of their country. They were also aware that Dickens, as the most popular author of the day, had the ear of the entire English-speaking world. His opinion would become the most widely known and undo the damage done by other British travellers. With the publication of *American Notes*, the Americans were mortified to learn that Dickens's opinion, too, was an unfavourable one. Far from redressing the Tory view, he had endorsed it. In reply to a letter of congratulation on his book from Mrs. Trollope, Dickens said that her praise was all the more valuable to him because he thought that no writer had described America more entertainingly than she had. The cry of exaggeration that had been raised against both of them only proved the truth of their observations. This was a change of tune for Dickens. The Radical and the Tory had found common ground in an active dislike of America.

The Americans were also angry with Dickens because it seemed to them terribly ungrateful that he should have written an unfriendly book after having received so great a welcome. This attitude puzzled Dickens. He could not understand why the Americans should have expected him, who had criticised his own country so much, not to criticise theirs. He had said much harder things about Britain than he had said about America. Such intolerance of criticism disgusted him. By their reaction to *American Notes*, the Americans were to bring down on their own heads a terrible punishment—the American chapters of *Martin Chuzzlewit*.

The sales of the monthly parts of *Martin Chuzzlewit* were not going well, when Dickens decided, in June 1843, to send his hero to America. Commercially, this was a shrewd decision. To the British public the American was, by this time, an established figure of fun, and they enjoyed reading about him. But this was not the only reason why Dickens sent Martin to the United States. The uproar over *American Notes* was still going on in America. Dickens was still being calumnied in the Rowdy Press. Every mailboat from America brought him abusive letters. He was disgusted with the country, and in *Martin Chuzzlewit* he intended to give "the eagle a final poke under the fifth rib".

For Americans, reading *Martin Chuzzlewit* had the quality of a nightmare. All the faults of the national character, clothed in human form, were paraded before them like the seven deadly sins in a morality play—La Fayette Kettle, Colonel Diver, Jefferson Brick, General Choke, Hannibal Chollop, the Honourable Elijah Pogram—each grotesque caricature introduced as "one of the most remarkable men in our country, sir!" Nowhere in *Martin Chuzzlewit* is there a mention of the virtues described in *American Notes*. Dickens, writing at the height of his power, held up a mirror to the vulgar, boastful, philistine, smart-dealing America of the 1840s, the land of the almighty dollar. "The more of that worthless ballast, honour and fair-dealing, which any man cast over-board from the ship of his Good Name and Good Intent, the more ample stowage-room he had for dollars. Make commerce one huge lie and mighty theft. Deface the banner of the nation for an idle rag; pollute it star by star; and cut out stripe by stripe as from the arm of a degraded soldier. Do anything for dollars! What is a flag to *them*."

No other book, not even Mrs. Trollope's *Domestic Manners of the Americans*, had ever aroused the Americans to such a fury. "All Yankee-Doodle-dum," Carlyle wrote, "blazed up like one universal soda bottle." The Americans were angry at the satire of *Martin Chuzzlewit*, not because it was false but because it was true. Feeling against Dickens ran so high that he dared not travel to Liverpool to say goodbye to his friend Macready when the actor set sail for a tour of the United States. Dickens believed that his presence at the dock would be fatal to Macready's success.

Martin Chuzzlewit was still outraging the Americans and amusing the British as Barnum and Tom Thumb prepared to leave New York. When the public heard that Tom Thumb was going abroad they hurried to the American Museum to catch a last glimpse of him. Advertisements warned them that the opportunity of seeing the dwarf was rapidly slipping away. Barnum was determined to squeeze the last cent out of the public, and he exhibited Tom Thumb right up to the time of sailing. When their departure was delayed by easterly winds posters announced that "a few hours more remain for Tom Thumb to be seen at the American Museum". The dwarf remained on exhibition until one hour before the *Yorkshire* sailed. He was then escorted to the docks by a procession of ten thousand people, headed by the municipal brass band.

As the *Yorkshire* moved down the Hudson river Barnum waved goodbye to the crowds on the docks. Phineas Taylor Barnum—one of the most remarkable men in our country, sir!—was off to visit the unnat'ral old parent. This was a great moment for all Americans. Although they did not know it, a champion was setting forth to avenge all the condescension and mockery they had endured for so long at the hands of the British. Within two months of his arrival Barnum would have Queen Victoria, the aristocracy and the whole of London dancing to his tune, and that tune was "Yankee Doodle".

Chapter Four

YANKEE DOODLE COMES TO TOWN

AFTER A voyage of eighteen days the *Yorkshire* docked at Liverpool on Monday, 5 February, 1844. Barnum did not want anyone to see Tom Thumb before he made his London début, so the dwarf was smuggled ashore in his mother's arms. Barnum's feelings of relief at being once more on solid ground were soon dispelled by his first encounters with the British. He found them quite as well up on smart dealing as any American. In the Customs he was expected to pay duty on every article he could not swear was of British manufacture, and then he was obliged to tip six porters half a crown apiece, even though only half that number carried his luggage, the others acting as a guard of honour.

At the Waterloo Hotel he washed down his indignation with a bottle of port and dined on sirloin of beef and fried soles in shrimp sauce. He was in a better humour when he left the hotel to take a look at the town. A short walk brought him to the Nelson Monument and, as he stood gazing, a distinguished old gentleman approached him and offered to explain the various devices with which the monument was decorated. The encounter pleased Barnum. "I had heard much of the coldness and haughty bearing of the English people," he wrote, "and I was rejoiced to be able so soon to testify that they had been seriously slandered . . . Human nature rose at least a hundred degrees in my estimation as I reflected that an old English gentleman could at once be so wealthy and so kind and disinterested. I already expected every moment to be invited to spend a week at his mansion, and to ride about the city in his splendid equipage, and therefore I gave him

68

A drawing of the American Dwarf which appeared in the
Illustrated London News 24 February, 1844

Barnum's American Museum in New York

a parting bow of thanks, half ashamed that I had so long trespassed on his kindness, when he extended his hand, and in the voice of a mendicant remarked that he would be thankful for any remuneration I thought fit to bestow for his trouble!"

Another disappointment awaited Barnum back at the hotel, where the owner of a cheap waxworks show had called to see him. This showman had heard of the arrival of Tom Thumb and offered to engage him at two pounds a week. This offer, worth ten dollars, was so derisory that Barnum did not know how best to reply without hurting the man's feelings. He told him that he had no intention of exhibiting Tom Thumb for less than one shilling admission, the equivalent of the twenty-five cents he had charged in America. Moreover, he did not plan to exhibit Tom Thumb publicly until after the dwarf had had an audience with the Queen at Buckingham Palace. The showman replied that his offer was a generous one. The price of admission he would charge could be no more than three halfpence, because no one would pay more than that to see a dwarf. He also told Barnum that he could forget all about showing Tom Thumb to the Queen, because the Court was in mourning.

This piece of news upset Barnum's plans. "It had been my intention," he wrote, "to proceed directly to London and begin operations at 'headquarters'—that is, at the Palace, if possible. But I learned that the royal family was in mourning because of the death of Prince Albert's father, and would not permit the approach of entertainments. My letters of introduction speedily brought me into relations of friendship with many excellent families, and I was induced to hire a hall and present the General to the public in Liverpool for a short time."

Next morning Barnum received a note from Madame Celeste, manageress of the Theatre Royal, Liverpool, whom he had known in New York. She invited him to make use of her private box, so he went along to the theatre that evening with Tom Thumb concealed beneath his cloak. At the theatre the dwarf,

F   69

excited by what he saw on the stage below him, kept jumping in and out of Barnum's cloak. His lively behaviour attracted the attention of a lady and gentleman in an adjoining box and, during the interval, the lady remarked to Barnum on the intelligent interest his child took in the theatre. Barnum explained that this was not a child, but the famous American dwarf, General Tom Thumb. The couple were delighted by Tom Thumb, who had stepped completely out of Barnum's cloak to give them a good view of himself. They urged Barnum to take him to Manchester, where they lived. They assured him that an exhibition there would be very profitable. He asked them what price of admission they would recommend him to charge. The lady suggested that as the General was obviously a great curiosity, he might put it as high as twopence. But her husband corrected her and told Barnum to charge one penny, for that was the highest price anyone in Britain would pay to see a dwarf. "I could but laugh at the novelty of the joke," Barnum wrote, "and yet there was a sadness settling down upon me in the thought that dwarfs were at rather a low figure in the fancy-stocks of England."

Long before Barnum and Tom Thumb arrived, the exhibition of dwarfs had acquired a bad reputation in Britain. From the sixteenth century onwards they had been exhibited at fairs, inns and coffee-houses all over the country. These dwarfs were rarely perfect: they were clumsy, ugly creatures, with huge heads, massive torsos and short, twisted legs, like the one seen at a country fair in Scotland, and vividly described by James Hogg, the Ettrick Shepherd: "A wee dwarfie woman, no three feet high, wi' a husband sax feet four; I never saw a happier couple. She loupt until the pouch o' his shooting-jacket, and keekit out like a maukin. But oh! she had a great ugly wide mouth and her teeth were as sharp and yellow as prins. I wudna hae sleepit in the same bed wi' sic a vermin for the mines o' Peru, for gin she had f'an upon a body in the middle of the nicht, and fastened on their throats like a rotten, there wad hae been nae shakin' her aff—the vampire. She was in the family way." Such exhibitions did not command a great following among the educated sections of the public.

Apart from their repulsive nature, there was another reason why these exhibitions had become discredited. Showmen made extravagant claims for their dwarfs, and exhibitions often ended in uproar, for the dwarfs were seldom as small as advertised. Some advertisements were the work of practical jokers. In 1749 it was announced that a dwarf small enough to get into a wine bottle would appear at the Haymarket Theatre, and a great audience assembled to witness the feat. A host of similar advertisements followed, among them one for Signor Capitello Jumpedo, lately arrived from Italy, "a surprising dwarf, no taller than a common tavern tobacco-pipe, who can perform many wonderful equilibres on the slack or tight rope; likewise he will transform his body in above ten thousand different shapes and postures; and after he has diverted the spectators two hours and a half, he will open his mouth wide and jump down his own throat". Surprisingly enough, many people turned up at the time and place announced.

By the nineteenth century the dwarf had become recognised as a medical phenomenon, and more and more people stayed away, as they realised that what they were being asked to watch was often nothing more than the antics of a hydrocephalic cretin. The squalid industrial towns of Britain swarmed with such creatures, blind, stunted and idiotic. To exhibit them was held by many to be an affront to a civilised society, whose energies should be used to abolish the conditions that caused such unfortunates to be born.

Tom Thumb was different from these dwarfs. Strictly speaking, he was not a dwarf but a midget, a Lilliputian, a perfectly formed miniature man. Most dwarfs left a disagreeable impression behind them, but Tom Thumb was pleasant, if a shade elfin, to look upon. He did not distress his audiences, nor could they feel sorry for him, for he was such a happy, intelligent little fellow. As Barnum thought of the differences between Tom Thumb and the usual run of misshapen dwarfs, his confidence returned. To the couple from Manchester, he declared magniloquently, "Never shall the price be less than one shilling sterling, and some of the nobility and gentry of England will yet pay gold to see General Tom Thumb!"

These were brave words, for Barnum had no plans for achieving the support of the nobility; indeed, he had no plans of any kind. He had been so confident of gaining an audience with the Queen that he had left New York without making advance arrangements for the exhibition of Tom Thumb in London. Now that the chances of a royal audience were remote he was forced to make preparations for a less illustrious event—the presentation of Tom Thumb to the people of Liverpool.

An advertisement announcing Tom Thumb's first public appearance in Britain appeared in all the Liverpool papers

TOM THUMB ARRIVED!
CHARLES S. STRATTON, known as
GENERAL TOM THUMB, Jun.,
THE AMERICAN DWARF!

Is happy to announce to the Ladies and Gentlemen of Liverpool that he has arrived, in good health and spirits, from his native land, and will have the honour of making his first appearance before a British Public tomorrow, (Saturday), the 10th instant, at the PORTICO, BOLD STREET, where he may be seen for a few days only.

GENERAL TOM THUMB, Jun., is twelve years old, TWENTY-FIVE INCHES HIGH, and
WEIGHS ONLY FIFTEEN POUNDS!!

That having been his precise weight when only six months old. He is of fine symmetrical proportions, very graceful and manly in his manners; lively, sociable and intelligent. He will amuse his Visitors with a variety of Songs, Dances, etc.

TOM THUMB, Jun., was visited in America by more

than HALF A MILLION of Ladies and Gentlemen of the highest distinction, who universally pronounced him the Greatest Natural Curiosity in the World. He is, beyond all question, the SMALLEST PERSON that ever WALKED ALONE!

As in all his promotions, Barnum was relying on the Press to whip up the interest of the public. In America he had always insisted on publicity in the editorial columns in return for taking out advertising space, but the Liverpool editors were reluctant to do this. Barnum consoled himself with the thought that Liverpool was a provincial city, and here one could not expect to find editors of the calibre of Bennett of the *New York Herald* and Locke of the *New York Sun*. He would have to be content until he reached the sophisticated metropolis, where he was certain that the outlook of the editors would be as broad and flexible as that of their New York colleagues.

Tom Thumb's exhibition was poorly attended. The people of Liverpool did not take kindly to being asked to pay twelve times the usual price of admission to see a dwarf. One evening, after the rest of the audience had left, a man stayed behind to talk to Barnum. He was short and stout, with marked Hebraic features, and a large cigar protruded from under his prominent nose. His name was John Medex Maddox, and he was the manager of the Princess's Theatre, London, where he was offering a mixed bill of farce, vaudeville and Italian opera. He was looking for a novelty to divert the audience during the intervals, and he proposed to Barnum that Tom Thumb should appear for three nights at his theatre.

This was hardly the most auspicious manner in which to make a London début, but Barnum thought it best to accept Maddox's offer, for he could think of no other way of getting a London audience for Tom Thumb.

Tom Thumb made his first London appearance at the Princess's

73

Theatre, Oxford Street, on Tuesday, 20 February, 1844. The programme included Mr. and Mrs. Keeley in a farce entitled *Blasé* and Donizetti's *Don Pasquale* sung by a British company. The dwarf made his début during the interval between the second and third acts of the opera, watched from the wings by the cast dressed as jewellers, hairdressers, milliners and serenaders. The ballet girls chattered among themselves as they watched the antics of the dwarf on the stage. They were wearing the transparent gauze costume introduced to London by Taglioni, the Italian ballerina. To Barnum's puritanical mind, they were so scantily covered that they might just as well have been stark naked. Such dresses would not have been tolerated in America.

There were plenty of people in Britain who were equally horrified by the dress and dancing of the ballet girls, but they were not usually to be found among the audience at a London theatre, and it is doubtful if there were many present that night at the Princess's Theatre. For the most part, the audience was a rabble of all the disreputable elements in London—aristocratic bloods, soldiers, medical students and the ubiquitous "gents", that new emerging class of clerks and shop assistants who tried to live and dress like dandies on less than fifty pounds a year. The theatre swarmed with prostitutes of every kind. Prostitutes congregated in the New York theatres, but there they were confined to the gallery or "third tier"; in London theatres they filled the foyers and passages between acts, and solicited shamelessly. Some parts of the Princess's Theatre were no better than a brothel, and it was the same at every theatre in London.

Apart from a few bawdy remarks, Tom Thumb was received well enough by the audience, although he did not create the sensation Barnum was hoping for. But when Barnum considered how the audience had received the rest of the programme he had some reason to be satisfied. The entire evening was interrupted by whistles, catcalls and yells. Audiences in America

were rowdy enough, but he had never met with any that compared in coarseness and brutality to this one. During the most
amusing parts of the farce and the tenderest arias in the opera
some rude or obscene expression was shouted from the auditorium
in a stentorian voice. This was followed either by laughter and
approval or by a rain of blows on the head of the offender, who
was then expelled by being passed over the heads of the audience
to the nearest exit. At times there was absolute tumult and dis-
order. No one could hear the actors and singers, who went
imperviously about their parts on a stage strewn with apple
cores, orange peel and empty bottles. It was an audience without
taste or manners, vulgar and licentious, whose attention could
only be held, if held at all, by novelty and spectacle.

When Barnum came to London, theatre audiences demanded
variety in their entertainment, and there was no lack of managers
willing to pander to their taste with a never-ending stream of
melodramas, farces, operas and burlesques produced in mixed
bills of various combinations. It was not unusual for a theatre to
put on as many as twenty-five productions in a year, together
with an extravaganza at Easter and a pantomime at Christmas.
Audiences were fickle, and managers were constantly on the
look-out for fresh novelties with which to divert them. These
efforts to attract audiences had led to bitter rivalry between
theatres, and the greatest casualty in the struggle was the legitimate
drama.

Up to the previous year, 1843, legitimate drama (five-act
tragedy and comedy without the introduction of music) could
be performed only in the three major theatres, Drury Lane,
Covent Garden and the Haymarket. In all other theatres, "minors"
as they were known, no legitimate drama was permitted, and no
performer was allowed to open his mouth on the stage without the
accompaniment of music. The law was broken nightly by the
convention of the "burletta", a play with music, which enabled
the minor theatres to put on any legitimate drama simply by

introducing a little incidental music and giving the characters a song or two to sing.

For the most part, however, the minor theatres had renounced legitimate drama and gone in for farce, melodrama, burlesque and extravaganza. These had proved so popular that two of the major theatres, Covent Garden and Drury Lane, were forced to provide the same fare in order to fill their vast auditoriums. And in one respect Covent Garden and Drury Lane had a great advantage over the minor theatres. Because of their vast size, the productions were more spectacular. To provide this spectacle, they went beyond the traditions of the theatre to those of the circus. In one production at Covent Garden a stage coach, pulled by six horses, rumbled full tilt round the stage, and in another elephants, ostriches and Burma bulls marched in procession. An oriental extravaganza at Drury Lane had animals from a Paris menagerie as the principal performers.

Many people had blamed the monopoly of the major theatres for the prostitution of drama, and when this monopoly was abolished, in 1843, by the Theatres Act they believed that the right now given to the minor theatres to perform legitimate drama would usher in a golden age for the English stage. As Planché wrote,

> *Sheridan now at Islington may shine,*
> *Marylebone echo "Marlowe's mighty line";*
> *Otway may raise the waters Lambeth yields,*
> *And Farquhar sparkle in St. George's Fields;*
> *Whycherley, flutter a Whitechapel pit,*
> *And Congreve wake all "Westminster to wit".*

But these hopes were not fulfilled, for the major and the minor theatres continued to provide the mixture as before. When Barnum came to London the only major theatre providing legitimate drama was the tiny Haymarket. Drury Lane and Covent Garden were in the hands of charlatans.

Alfred Bunn had replaced Macready as manager of Drury Lane. Coming at a time when the British theatre was in a low state, Bunn debased it still further. His policy was to give the public what they wanted. He followed Macready's season at Drury Lane with a season of Italian opera, spectacularly mounted and indifferently sung. The translations of the libretti, by Bunn himself, were so weak that *Punch* described them as "undone into English".

Covent Garden, too, had ceased to play drama, and the great theatre was rented by Monsieur Jullien for his promenade concerts. Jullien was a man of mystery; no one knew his background. It was said that he had been a waiter in a café and a bandsman in a regiment. He was certainly a superb showman. The public wanted something new and unusual, and he gave them this with special compositions designed for an orchestra unsurpassed in the number of its players, and a percussion section reinforced with explosives and fireworks. Every detail of his performance was extravagant. He conducted in a magnificent evening dress with white waistcoat and frilled shirt front. At the beginning of the concert a liveried footman offered him a silver tray bearing a jewelled baton and white kid gloves. Facing the audience, Jullien ostentatiously pulled the gloves over his hands, then picking up the baton, turned to the orchestra. His conducting was dramatic. At the quieter passages he danced on tiptoe, softly soothing his players with outstretched palm. Nearing a crescendo, he drove the orchestra furiously with whirling baton and wild gesticulations. At the conclusion he sank back exhausted into a gilt and velvet chair.

The minor theatres, too, had their share of adventurers, among them John Medex Maddox, manager of the Princess's Theatre. Maddox was notoriously close with money, and his actors often had to go to law before they got their salaries out of him. In the London theatre world there was a fund of stories about his meanness. It was said that the jobbing author he employed to provide the lighter pieces for his ever-changing bills was kept chained by his leg to the desk in a little room at the theatre, and for a meagre salary was compelled to produce at least two new farces a week.

Before taking over the Princess's Theatre in Oxford Street Maddox had kept the tobacconist's shop immediately opposite. This shop was now run by his brother, and during the day Maddox was usually to be found there, sitting on a barrel or lounging against the counter. He had the greatest respect for his brother's judgement, and always asked his advice before booking an entertainment. A theatre manager in the 1840s needed all the advice he could get, for running a theatre was often no more than a constant effort to make ends meet. The careers of many managers ended in disaster and despair, but Maddox was a natural born survivor. To make his theatre pay he would try anything. He was tireless in his search for novelties that might divert the public, but he was not too happy about the reception of his latest one, General Tom Thumb, the American Dwarf.

Tom Thumb made his second appearance at the Princess's Theatre on Friday, 23 February. The opera was Bellini's *I Puritani*, and the dwarf appeared on the stage between the second and third acts. Again Tom Thumb's reception failed to please Maddox. The dwarf made his third and final appearance there on Tuesday, 27 February. Maddox had taken care to give the audience an exceptionally strong bill. The opera was again *Don Pasquale*—always a great favourite, full of good tunes with a splendid opportunity for low comedy in the role of the notary—and, in addition to *Blasé*, two new farces were to be performed. The jobbing author had had a busy weekend.

The following day Maddox was in his brother's shop discussing future programmes. They talked of the productions of *La Sonambula* and *Norma* that were to be presented later in the week. They doubted if *Blasé* could be given yet another performance without the public suspecting that old goods were being foisted upon them. They discussed the forthcoming extravaganza at

Easter, when the public always expected something special, and Maddox wondered how spectacular he could afford to make it this year. They did not mention Tom Thumb. Absorbed in the daily problems of running a theatre, they had already forgotten about the dwarf.

Tom Thumb's failure at the Princess's Theatre did not worry Barnum unduly. He was certain that if he could present the dwarf properly in his own time and in his own way there was every chance of having a great success. He was more concerned with his inability so far to arouse the interest of the London Press. The first thing he had done on arriving in London had been to take Tom Thumb on a round of visits to newspaper editors, but apart from the *Illustrated London News*, none of the other newspapers considered the dwarf worth a mention in their columns. The London editors, like their Liverpool colleagues, did not deal in sensationalism. Barnum now realised that there was no Rowdy Press in Britain. The newspapers and periodicals were read almost exclusively by the middle and the upper classes, and gave only a sober presentation of the news.

Newspapers had always played a crucial part in his publicity campaigns. Without the help of the Press, he felt as if he were fighting with both arms tied behind his back. He believed it vital to get some newspaper publicity, for he knew of no other means that would enable him to exploit his dwarf fully. Even Tom Thumb's performance at the Princess's Theatre had excited no comment in the Press beyond a brief sentence in the *Illustrated London News*, which stated, "The production of this little monster affords another melancholy proof of the *low* state the legitimate drama has been reduced to!" Barnum knew that if he were to repeat in London the success he had had with Tom Thumb in New York he must think of some way of getting the newspapers interested in his dwarf.

He also knew that the Princess's Theatre had not been the best place to present Tom Thumb. The vast middle classes, whose shillings he sought, did not patronise theatres. Some forward-looking theatre managers, who also realised this, were soon to start putting their houses in order. Stalls were to be introduced to divide the respectable from the vulgar; highly priced and reservable, they attracted the middle classes. The prostitutes were to be told to go about their business more discreetly. The theatre finally achieved respectability in the 1850s, when the Queen became a regular patron. This royal example, more than any other reason, caused the middle classes to flock to the theatre.

For many years prior to the accession of Queen Victoria the only example set by the British monarchy had been one of profligacy. Now the country had a young Queen who set an example in all that was best and good, and her subjects were happy to follow her in everything she did. It was this tendency of the British people to follow the example of their Queen that made Barnum so anxious to obtain her patronage for Tom Thumb, but with the Court in mourning for the death of Prince Albert's father there seemed little chance of the Queen receiving the dwarf. Barnum, however, still hoped for a royal audience, and with this in mind he called on Edward Everett, United States Minister to the Court of St. James's.

Barnum carried a letter of introduction to Edward Everett from Horace Greeley, editor of the *New York Tribune*, and "to that letter," he said, "perhaps more than anything else, I was indebted for my first introduction to Her Majesty". At first sight Edward Everett would seem to be the last sort of person to further the interests of a showman and his dwarf. He was one of the most distinguished American scholars of his day. He had been appointed Latin Tutor at Harvard at eighteen years of age, and five years later the same university elected him Professor of Greek Language and Literature. His political career had been equally brilliant. After his election to Congress he was Governor of Massachusetts for four successive terms. He had travelled in Europe and met all the leading political and literary figures. In 1841, at the age of forty-seven, he was appointed United States Minister to the Court of St. James's. His diplomatic duties still left him time for his academic pursuits. He lectured on a wide range of subjects to many learned institutions. He had long been planning a great work on some broad question and had selected The Law of Nations, a treatise on the matters discussed between the governments of the United States and Europe since the peace of 1793.

A young American lawyer, Maunsell B. Field, who called on Everett about the same time as Barnum, wrote, "I found Mr. Everett as frigid as an iceberg. He was as polished as his own writings, but equally cold. To a young man just out of college, this sort of reception operated like a wet blanket. After my first call, I never ventured upon him again. I feared taking cold." But much of Everett's icy reserve was caused by his shyness. Tom Thumb completely disarmed him. His heart warmed to his diminutive countryman, and he invited Barnum and the dwarf to dine with him and his family.

When the question of a royal audience was raised Everett did not dismiss the idea out of hand. True, the Court was in mourning for Duke Ernest of Saxe-Coburg-Gotha. Victoria and Albert had wept like children when they heard of his death. Everett remarked that they must have forgotten the nuisance the old Duke had been to them during his lifetime. He had broken up Albert's home by his licentious behaviour. He had schemed to get Victoria to settle an allowance on him. He had insulted them both for not calling their eldest son after him. His death must have been a relief to the royal couple. An audience for Tom Thumb was still a possibility, and Everett promised Barnum that he would use his influence at the Palace.

Now that Everett had revived in him the hope of a royal audience for Tom Thumb, Barnum was reluctant to exhibit the dwarf publicly until he had acquired the cachet that the Queen's patronage would give him. In the meantime, while waiting for the summons to the Palace, he set about securing the next best thing, the patronage of the aristocracy.

Barnum calculated that the best way to gain the interest of the aristocracy was to appear to be on equal terms with them. His first step was to rent a furnished house in Grafton Street, previously occupied by Lord Talbot. From this stylish address, he sent invitations to members of the aristocracy to a series of private receptions by General Tom Thumb. Not all of those invited came to the first reception, but those who did were very much taken with the dwarf. The word went round, and a greater number came to the next reception, among them some who had not been invited. These were turned away at the door. This procedure was part of Barnum's plan. "I had not yet announced a public exhibition," he wrote, "and as a private American gentleman it became me to maintain the dignity of my position. I therefore instructed my servant, dressed in the tinselled and powdered style of England, to deny admission to my mansion to see my 'ward', excepting to persons who brought cards of invitation. He did it in a proper manner, and no offence could be taken—though I was always particular to send an invitation immediately to such as had not been admitted."

Barnum knew his plan was working when the Baroness Rothschild asked him to bring Tom Thumb to a private party she was giving at her house in Piccadilly. The Baroness, not quite certain of their status, sent her carriage for them. This was driven not to the back door, usually reserved for entertainers, but through the main gates and up to the front entrance. In the brilliantly illuminated hall they were received by half a dozen footmen, so elegantly dressed that Barnum mistook them for some of the guests. "As we entered the drawing-room," he wrote, "a glare of magnificence met my sight which it is impossible for me to describe. The Baroness was seated on a gorgeous couch covered with rich figured silk damask (there were several similar couches in the room), and several lords and ladies were seated in chairs elegantly carved and covered with gold, looking indeed like solid gold, except the bottoms, which were of rich velvet . . . The immense chandeliers, candelabras, etc., exceeded all my powers of description; and I confess my total inability to give a correct idea of the splendor in which lived the wife of the most wealthy banker in the world."

Here Barnum and Tom Thumb spent about two hours. "On taking our leave," Barnum wrote, "an elegant and well-filled purse was quietly slipped into my hand, and I felt that the golden shower was beginning to fall!" So discreetly was this done that Barnum could almost have fancied it to be a delusion had not precisely the same thing happened to him a few nights later at the mansion of Mr. Drummond, another eminent banker.

Then came a letter from Everett inviting Barnum and Tom Thumb to breakfast. The third guest was to be the Honourable Charles Augustus Murray, Master of the Queen's Household.

Unlike most British aristocrats, Murray was sympathetic towards America. He liked meeting Americans. In London he sought them out. Murray was thirty-seven years old. He was the second son of the Baron Dunmore of Dunmore, a member of one of the most ancient Scottish families. He was distinguished for his scholarship, good looks and magnificent physique. For two years he had travelled widely in the United States. He was not only familiar with the settled part of the country but had also penetrated the unexplored wilderness to the west—a land of rivers, mountains, canyons, forests and prairies. This was the land of the Indian, who was being rapidly overtaken, exploited and corrupted by the advance of the white man. In two romances, *Pioneer* and *The Last of the Mohicans*, published in the 1820s, James Fenimore Cooper had told of the high moral qualities and dauntless courage of the Red Indian. These books were widely read not only in America but also in Europe, where the imagination had long been fired by the ideal of the Noble Savage, uncorrupted by western civilisation. The novels of Cooper had struck a responsive chord in Murray's heart, and while in America he hoped to meet some Indians. His chance came at Fort Leavenworth when a band of one hundred and fifty Pawnees rode out of the wilderness. Murray was impressed by their natural dignity and intuitive tact. He arranged to travel with them when they returned to their tribe. After a fortnight's hard ride to the west they overtook the tribe camped in six hundred lodges on a wide prairie.

For more than a year Murray lived with the Pawnees in the wilderness. He hunted buffalo with them and fought with them against the Cheyenne. He studied their customs and their manners. Then, in the middle of August 1836, he left them and travelled eastwards across hundreds of miles of trackless wilderness to Fort Leavenworth. His admiration for the Indian had been modified by his stay with them. There were certain points concerning their ethics and personal behaviour to which Cooper had given no prominence in his romances. The Indian camps were abominably filthy. Every article inside the lodges was covered with vermin. The dignity and repose of the Indians was an act they put on only in the presence of white men. Among themselves they were rowdy and licentious. But Murray was not completely disillusioned about Indians, for although he knew their vices, he also knew their virtues. The Indians were brave and steadfast, patient of pain and fatigue, and of all the virtues in the world, these were the ones he admired most.

On his return to London in 1838, Murray was appointed Master of the Queen's Household to the young Queen Victoria, then only eighteen years old. The following year he published his *Travels in North America*. Of all the books written on America by British travellers, Murray's was one of the few favourable accounts. Whenever he found shortcomings in America he looked for an explanation. An example of this is seen in his remarks on Louisville, which he describes as "active and thriving, but like all others in the West, wretchedly lighted and paved *at present*".

Above Barnum training Tom Thumb
Below The fight with the poodle at Buckingham Palace

Tom Thumb dressed as Napoleon

Then he goes on, "It is necessary to mark these two words, as in this most wonderful continent, observations of a condemnatory nature are not likely to be true for more than twelve months."

At the time of Murray's visit the population of Louisville was under eleven thousand: thirty years later the population was over one hundred thousand. Few British travellers had been willing to make this kind of allowance for the constant change and rapid growth of America. Mrs. Trollope, discussing the lack of social amenities in Cincinnati compared to those in London and Paris, did not mention that thirty years earlier an Indian camp had occupied the same site.

On a morning in March, 1844, Murray found himself sitting down to breakfast with three disparate Americans—an ambassador, a showman and a dwarf. Before meeting Murray, Barnum had taken care to read *Travels in North America*, and he told him how much he admired his opinion of the American people. But Barnum was astute enough to know that flattery alone would get him nowhere with such a polished courtier, so he came right out and told Murray how important an audience with Queen Victoria was to the success of his show, and that, if he did not get one soon, then he was packing his traps and going to Paris, where he was sure King Louis Philippe wouldn't pass up the chance of seeing Tom Thumb. No, sir! This Yankee directness delighted Murray. Moreover, he was charmed by Tom Thumb, and thought it likely that the dwarf would amuse the Queen. Nor could he think of a more fitting person to divert a Queen than a dwarf, for dwarfs had long been the privileged companions of royalty. The legendary Tom Thumb himself had been a member of King Arthur's Court. And now a latter-day Tom Thumb at the Court of Queen Victoria. Murray was amused at the conceit. Buckingham Palace was a gloomy place at the moment, and Tom Thumb would be just the person to distract the Queen and Prince Albert from their difficult efforts to find something good to say about the late Prince Ernest. Besides, they would certainly want to see the dwarf before Louis Philippe did. So Murray hinted to Barnum that something perhaps might be arranged and then changed the conversation to other topics.

After a week had passed without any word from Murray about the audience with the Queen, Barnum decided to go ahead with the arrangements for the public exhibition of Tom Thumb. He could not afford to keep up the Grafton Street establishment indefinitely. Moreover, he now had reason to believe that the aristocracy would support an exhibition, and he was confident that the middle classes would follow the example of their betters. He had spent a lot of money promoting Tom Thumb in high society. The dwarf was now the darling of the fashionable world, but Barnum did not want the aristocracy to monopolise him. The "golden shower" that had started at the Baroness Rothschild's continued to fall at other private parties, but Barnum knew that a steady downpour of shillings from the public counted most. So he hired a room at the Egyptian Hall in Piccadilly.

The Egyptian Hall was the most famous exhibition hall in London; it was also one of the most fantastic buildings in the metropolis. The façade, which was copied from the Temple of Tentyra, was decorated with enormous figures of Isis and Osiris. It was the masterpiece of Peter Frederick Robinson, an architect who had already made a reputation with Norman villas, Tudor parsonages and Swiss cottages. Built in 1812, and originally intended as a natural history museum, it was soon given over to exhibitions and entertainments. Napoleon's coach had been seen there, and a family of Laplanders, and a model of the field of Waterloo, and Benjamin Robert Haydon's enormous painting of *Christ's Entry into Jerusalem*. It had been the scene of innumerable one-man shows, lectures, panoramas and dioramas. The Egyptian Hall contained three exhibition rooms, the largest of these, known as "the great room", was on the ground floor. Upstairs, two smaller rooms gave off on either side of the first-floor landing. One of these rooms was booked by Barnum. He would have preferred the great room downstairs, but this was already taken by his fellow countryman, George Catlin, who was exhibiting his North American Indian Collection.

After completing his business with the proprietress of the Egyptian Hall, Barnum called in to pay his respects to George Catlin. He pushed open the door of the great room and found himself back in America, but not the America he knew. Every inch of wall space was covered by six hundred paintings made during Catlin's seven years of travel among the Red Indians. There were portraits of distinguished chiefs and warriors; paintings of the various tribes hunting, fighting and dancing; landscapes of river, mountain, forest and prairie. This tremendous gallery of Indian life contained more than three thousand figures, the costumes, weapons and features all accurately depicted.

Also on view were many of the costumes and weapons worn when the portraits were painted, and, in addition, more than five hundred other Indian artifacts, ranging from children's rattles to scalping knives. In the middle of the room stood a splendid wigwam from the country of the Crows, twenty-five feet high, covered by twenty buffalo skins ornamented and embroidered with porcupine quills, supported by thirty poles and capable of sheltering eighty people.

This comprehensive collection had been put together by one man, George Catlin. He had realised that the rapid destruction of the Indians by the white man, through war, disease and alcohol, would soon cause all traces of them to be lost, so he determined to gain knowledge of their manners and customs and draw exact reproductions of their features. And he was barely in time, for some of the Indian nations had been reduced to scattered remnants or had disappeared altogether. Catlin spent seven years among the Indians with the sole purpose of perfecting his collection. He had paddled his canoe and led his packhorse through the wilderness to the wildest and remotest tribes. Every item had been gathered and every painting had been made on the spot, often at the risk of his life.

After exhibiting his Indian Collection in New York, Boston and Philadelphia, Catlin brought it to London. Charles Augustus Murray, who had travelled with Catlin on the Mississippi, encouraged him to do this and arranged for its exhibition at the Egyptian Hall. Since 1840 Catlin's North American Indian Collection had been a popular feature of the London scene, and for the past two years his exhibition had been made even more interesting by nine Ojibbeway Indians from the southern shores of Lake Superior. Against the background of the Collection, the Ojibbeways gave a demonstration of war dances.

Barnum's visit to the Egyptian Hall coincided with a great disappointment for Catlin. That week the Ojibbeways had defected to another manager. They were no longer willing to perform in Catlin's Indian Collection, and Barnum found the great room empty of visitors.

Catlin explained to him that this sudden breakup with the Ojibbeways, coming as it did, at the start of the fashionable season, was a disaster, for he now had the great room at the Egyptian Hall, at a heavy rent, left on his hands for three more months. With the departure of the Indians the excitement had gone from his exhibition, which had already been more than three years in the same building. That week there had scarcely been enough visitors to meet expenses, and he had spent most of his time in an adjoining office, where he had started to get together a book, a large illustrated work to be entitled *Catlin's Hunting Scenes and Amusements of the North American Indians*. As he reckoned that several months would be necessary for the completion of this work, he decided to keep his collection in the great room, as it was, until the expiration of his lease, and then pack it up and return to America.

When Barnum heard this he immediately made a proposal to Catlin: that if the exhibition of Tom Thumb were a success and the upstairs room proved to be too small, then Catlin should sub-let the great room to Barnum for the remainder of his tenancy. The Indian Collection could remain in position until Catlin was ready to pack it up. Catlin, delighted at the thought of being relieved of the rent of the great room, yet still being allowed to keep his collection in it, agreed at once to Barnum's proposal.

Barnum was to move Tom Thumb into Catlin's room sooner than he had hoped, for barely had his exhibition opened than a Life Guard rode up Grafton Street and brought him a note conveying the long-awaited invitation from the Queen to General Tom Thumb and his guardian, Mr. Barnum, to appear before her on Saturday evening, March 23. Determined to make the most of the occasion, Barnum put a placard on the door of the Egyptian Hall: "Closed this evening, General Tom Thumb being at Buckingham Palace by command of Her Majesty."

Chapter Five

THE COURT DWARF

AT BUCKINGHAM PALACE Barnum and Tom Thumb were met by Charles Augustus Murray, who told them that the Queen wanted the dwarf to appear before her exactly as he would appear anywhere else. He then handed them over to a Lord in Waiting. Barnum wrote, "We were conducted through a long corridor to a broad flight of marble steps, which led to the Queen's magnificent picture gallery, where her Majesty and Prince Albert, the Duchess of Kent, and twenty or thirty of the nobility, were awaiting our arrival. They were standing at the farther end of the room when the doors were thrown open, and the General toddled in, looking like a wax doll gifted with the power of locomotion. Surprise and pleasure were depicted on the countenances of the royal circle, at beholding this *mite* of humanity so much smaller than they had evidently expected to find him."

Tom Thumb advanced with a firm step and, making a graceful bow, said, "Good evening, *Ladies and Gentlemen!*" A burst of laughter followed this salutation.

The Queen stepped forward and took Tom Thumb by the hand. Together they strolled about the room. The dwarf admired the decorations and pronounced some of the paintings to be "first-rate". The Queen was delighted with the dwarf. Again and again she laughed at the drollness of his remarks. "The Queen was modestly attired in plain black, and wore no ornaments," Barnum wrote. "Indeed, surrounded as she was by ladies arrayed in the highest style of magnificence, their dresses sparkling with diamonds, a stranger would have selected her as the last person in the circle who could have been the Queen of England."

Tom Thumb asked after the health of the Prince of Wales and said he would like to meet him. The Queen replied that the Prince was in bed, but that he should see him on some future occasion. She was not offended by Tom Thumb's familiarity. In times past a dwarf had always held a privileged position in the courts of Europe. His role, like that of the jester, was to amuse the king, to dispel his melancholy and to help him forget for a short while the cares of state. A dwarf was allowed to be familiar with the king, and was never expected to be servile. There had been no court dwarf in England since the death of Coppernin, dwarf to George II, but Queen Victoria knew instinctively how to behave towards one, just as Tom Thumb naturally assumed the role he could have played in the courts of Europe since earliest times.

He could have been in the retinue of Tiberius. Augustus, who had dwarfs sent to him from all corners of the earth, would have welcomed him into his palace. He could have stood by the side of William the Conqueror as he embarked for England. He could have held the bridle of the Emperor Otho's horse in state processions. He could have been the companion of Spanish kings. His portrait could have been painted by Domenchino, Raphael or Velasquez.

At no point during his audience with Queen Victoria did Tom Thumb play his role more perfectly than when, after a stay of more than an hour, the time came to leave. The Lord in Waiting had previously instructed Barnum and the dwarf to back out of the royal presence, keeping their faces always towards the Queen. The pace at which Barnum backed out was too fast for Tom Thumb and, whenever the dwarf found he was losing ground, he turned round, ran a few steps until he caught up, then faced towards the Queen again and walked backwards. As they had a considerable distance to travel in the long gallery before reaching the door, he continued this method of catching up until the room rang again and again with laughter. Tom Thumb was aware that he cut a comic figure, but the sight of the running dwarf annoyed the Queen's poodle, which barked at him and, to his dismay, made for his legs. The dwarf attacked the dog with his little cane, and this grotesque combat caused even more amusement. When Tom Thumb had left the gallery the Queen sent one of the royal party to express the hope that he had suffered no harm from the poodle, and the Lord in Waiting added that in the event of injury to so renowned a personage he should fear a declaration of war by the United States.

"The courtesies of the Palace were not yet exhausted," Barnum wrote, "for we were escorted to an apartment in which refreshments had been provided for us. We did ample justice to the viands, though my mind was rather looking into the future than enjoying the present." He was anxious that the newspapers should carry the news of Tom Thumb's audience. He knew that all the leading papers published the Court Circular and, on enquiry, he was told that the editor of the Circular was, at that moment, in the Palace. The editor was sent for, and Barnum asked him if a report of the audience could be inserted. The editor was puzzled. The Court Circular mentioned all distinguished visitors to the Palace, but should an American dwarf, even one with such a high military rank, be listed alongside peers of the realm, ambassadors and ministers of the crown? To resolve his dilemma, he suggested to Barnum that he write out whatever he wished to be printed. Barnum did this, and his report of the audience was printed verbatim. On Monday morning people read in their newspapers that "the American Dwarf, General Tom Thumb, accompanied by his guardian, Mr. P. T. Barnum of New York, had the honour of attending the Palace on Saturday evening, when the General exhibited his clever imitations of Napoleon, etc., which elicited the approbation of Her Majesty and the Royal Circle".

Barnum had achieved not only the patronage of the Queen but also the newspaper publicity he believed essential to the success of his exhibition. Deprived of a Rowdy Press similar to the one in New York, he had gained entry into the most exclusive section of the London papers: he had succeeded in advertising a dwarf in the column reserved for the Queen of England and her Court.

Following the report in the Court Circular, there was a sharp increase in the number of people who came to the exhibition at the Egyptian Hall. The advertisements for Tom Thumb now stated that the dwarf was "Under the patronage of Her Majesty the Queen". The crowds could not all be accommodated in the upstairs room and, as arranged, Barnum took over "the great room" downstairs from George Catlin, most of whose Indian curiosities remained as adornments. As Barnum had predicted, the audience with the Queen had done the trick, and he was all set for a profitable season. Then, to his delight, before the week was out he was invited again to bring his dwarf to Buckingham Palace.

The Queen had asked Barnum and Tom Thumb to a second audience because she wanted her children to meet the dwarf. This time they were received in the Yellow Room, which, in Barnum's opinion, surpassed in splendour even the drawing room of the Baroness Rothschild. "It was hung with drapery of rich yellow satin damask," he wrote, "the couches, sofas and chairs being covered with the same material. The vases, urns and ornaments were all of modern patterns, and the most exquisite workmanship. The room was panelled in gold, and the heavy cornices beautifully carved and gilt. The tables, pianos, etc., were mounted with gold, inlaid with pearl of various hues, and of the most elegant devices."

Tom Thumb bowed to the Queen and remarked that "he had seen her before". He added, "I think this is a prettier room than the picture gallery; that chandelier is very fine."

The Queen took him by the hand and said she hoped he was very well. The dwarf replied that he was "first-rate".

The Prince of Wales, two-and-a-half-years old, was introduced to Tom Thumb. "How are you, Prince?" asked the dwarf amiably. Then standing beside the shy little boy, he remarked, "The Prince is taller than I am, but I *feel* as big as anybody"; and he strutted up and down the room like a peacock amid shouts of laughter. Then the Queen introduced the three-and-a-half-year-old Princess Royal, who was as precocious as her brother was backward. The dwarf led her to his elegant little sofa, which Barnum had brought along, and sat himself down beside her. It had always been the particular duty of the court dwarf to be a playmate for the royal children, and there was no trace of servility in Tom Thumb's manner as he played with the Prince of Wales and the Princess Royal under the eyes of their parents.

Encouraged by his previous experience with the editor of the Court Circular, Barnum submitted a lengthier account of the second audience than he had written of the first, and again it was printed in full. The final paragraph left the reader in no doubt as to how high Tom Thumb stood in the favour of the Queen:

"Her Majesty, at the conclusion of the entertainment, was pleased to present to the General, with her own hand, a superb souvenir of the most exquisite handicraft, manufactured of mother-of-pearl, and mounted with gold and precious stones. On one side are the crown and royal initials 'V.R.', and on the reverse bouquets of flowers in enamel and rubies. In addition to this splendid gift, Her Majesty subsequently presented the General with a beautiful gold pencil case with the initials of Tom Thumb, and his coat of arms engraved on the emerald surmounting the case accompanying the royal souvenir, with the expression of Her Majesty's high gratification at the versatile talents of the General, and also a compliment to Mr. Barnum, his guardian, on the aptness of his pupil. The General then made his *congé*, amidst the congratulations of the royal party."

"The British public was now fairly excited," Barnum wrote. "Not to have seen General Tom Thumb was voted to be decidedly unfashionable, and from the 20th of March until the 20th of July the levees of the little General at Egyptian Hall were continually crowded—the receipts averaging during the whole period about $500 per day, sometimes going considerably beyond that sum. At the fashionable hour between fifty and sixty carriages of the nobility have been counted at one time standing in front of our exhibition rooms in Piccadilly. Portraits of the little General were published in all the pictorial papers of the time. Polkas and quadrilles were named after him, and songs were sung in his praise."

The success of Tom Thumb's exhibition was proving the power of the Queen's example and, among the radical journals, *Punch* was quick to point out that as the potency of her example was so great, she should see to it that she always set a good one. It seemed to the radicals that in these critical days of industrial and political unrest the Queen in her yearning for a court dwarf was looking backwards to less democratic times. After the first royal audience *Punch* observed tartly, "It appears that the dwarf General Tom Thumb and his showman—'guardian' lisps the Court Circular— have been to Buckingham Palace, commanded thither by Her Majesty the Queen, whose admiration of genius, native or foreign, has passed into a proverb."

The second visit of Tom Thumb to Buckingham Palace was noted by *Punch* "with due gravity". That Her Majesty had again commanded the appearance of the dwarf was, in *Punch*'s opinion, only to be expected. "We had only to reflect upon the countless acts of patronage towards the arts and sciences—had only to remember a few of the numerous personal condescensions of the Queen towards men of letters, artists, and philosophers—to be assured that even Tom Thumb would be welcomed with that graceful cordiality which has heretofore made Buckingham Palace and Windsor Castle the homes of poetry and science. Continental monarchs stop short in their royal favours at full-grown authors and artists; but the enthusiasm of Her Majesty Queen Victoria, not content with showering all sorts of favours and rewards upon the literary and artistic spirits of her own country and age, lavishes with prodigal hand most delicate honours upon an American Tom Thumb, whose outstanding genius it is to measure in his boots five-and-twenty inches!"

Sir Robert Peel, the Prime Minister, was also among those who were disturbed by the Queen's interest in Tom Thumb. Considering the state of the country, he thought she was being indiscreet. From the days of the madness of George III until the death of William IV, the Crown had become more and more unpopular, but in 1837, with the accession of the young Victoria, this attitude had changed. Her very youth made the country feel protective towards her. Her marriage to Prince Albert of Saxe-Coburg-Gotha, in 1840, aroused tremendous enthusiasm among her subjects, as did the birth of the Princess Royal in 1841, and that of the Prince of Wales in 1842. But these years were ones of utter misery for the working classes, and the radicals were fond of contrasting the poverty in the industrial towns with the luxury in Buckingham Palace.

The young Queen was, by inclination, autocratic. She had no interest in the condition of the working classes. She had no sympathy for the Chartists, believing them to be led, or rather misled, by criminals and professional agitators. She could be kind to individuals, but she could not approve of the efforts of the workers to help themselves. She could be moved to pity when she came face to face with misery. When she heard that the death of two sailors at a Spithead review had driven the wife of one of them mad she sent money to both families. She was concerned when her poodle attacked Tom Thumb, and at each audience Barnum had to assure her that the dwarf was kindly treated. Yet she could set her heart against measures intended to limit the hours of factory workers, many of them children.

Punch made great play of the report in the Court Circular that the Queen had seen fit to present souvenirs to the dwarf "*with her own hands*". After mentioning that these souvenirs were now being exhibited by Barnum as an additional attraction at the Egyptian Hall, *Punch* concluded the attack with these words: "It having been suggested that the many presents of jewellery, plate, books, pictures, and other rare chattels, made by the Queen to the various men and women of genius of her country, would, if brought together, amaze the most credulous—such exhibition will take place at the very earliest opportunity. The mother-of-pearl souvenir and gold pencil case, presented by the Queen to Tom Thumb, will, we can assure our readers, form the most striking objects in the collection."

In the months that followed, *Punch* was to return to the attack again and again. Barnum was delighted by *Punch*'s interest. He never cared what the newspapers said about him, for he had always believed that any publicity was better than none. In this case *Punch* was giving him marvellous publicity by coupling Tom Thumb with the Queen of England. "He was an almost constant theme for the London *Punch*," Barnum wrote, "which served the General and myself up so daintily that it no doubt added vastly to our receipts."

The royal audiences were becoming so frequent that Barnum had a court suit made for Tom Thumb, an elegant brown silk-velvet coat, richly embroidered, white satin vest, white silk stockings and pumps, wig, cocked hat and dress sword. Thus attired, Tom Thumb appeared before the Queen for the third time on Friday, 19 April. When she saw him she clapped her hands with delight. It was as though Sir Jeffrey Hudson, court dwarf to Charles I, had stepped out of one of the paintings by Van Dyke that hung in the Palace.

The Queen asked the dwarf to sing his favourite song. He obliged with "Yankee Doodle", the song of the American Revolutionary War. This outrageous choice diverted her so much that for an instant it seemed probable that she would knight Tom Thumb on the spot, as Charles I, in a moment of frolic, had knighted Jeffrey Hudson.

The report of this audience in the Court Circular was again in the unmistakable style of Barnum. It read, in part, "The royal party conversed happily with the little hero, and asked him a number of questions. His shrewdness and witty readiness afforded them much amusement." After each visit to Buckingham Palace "a handsome *douceur*" was sent to Barnum by the Queen's command. "This, however," he admitted, "was the smallest part of the advantage derived from these interviews, as will be at once apparent to all who consider the force of Court example in England."

If proof were needed of the force of Court example in England, the Queen had provided it by making the exhibition of a dwarf the most popular attraction in London. This was an exhibition that was completely against the spirit of the times. By 1844 dwarfs had been relegated from the West End of London to country fairs. Respectable people considered such exhibitions to be distasteful. They believed that these monsters should be seen only by the eyes of medical men, not exposed to the morbid curiosity of the public. They expected an exhibition to be instructive, not sensational.

Educational exhibitions were a characteristic recreation of the period. As they were instructive, no one could be reproved for going to see them. Vast numbers of respectable people who were reluctant to visit the theatre because of the unruly and indecorous behaviour of the audience looked to the exhibitions for instruction and relaxation. Astute promoters, while careful to emphasise the educational content of their exhibitions, also made them as entertaining as they could. The degree to which they combined amusement and instruction was the measure of their success, for their audiences enjoyed being entertained all the more if they knew they were being educated at the same time. At Easter 1844 all the successful London exhibitions were of this kind, with the exception of Tom Thumb.

There was the Chinese Collection at Hyde Park Corner, an exhibition of Chinese dancers, musicians and oriental curios. As a special attraction at Easter a Feast of Lanterns was held, when the salon was decorated with a great number of variegated lanterns, which gave an enchanting effect when lighted.

There was the Polytechnic, in Upper Regent Street, a scientific exhibition, with a diving bell within a huge glass tank, where members of the audience could be submerged and experience the not unpleasant sensation of pressure inside their heads; and a diver who sat at the bottom of the tank, and rapped his helmet playfully with the coppers that had been thrown to him; and half globes, brass pillars and water troughs so charged with electricity that they nearly dislocated the arms of those that touched them; and a microscope in which infinitesimal creatures in a drop of Thames water appeared like prehistoric monsters locked in combat.

There was Madame Tussaud's Waxworks, in Baker Street, a nicely balanced collection of heroes and villains. The latest additions were Commissioner Lin, the execrated foe in the recent Anglo-Chinese imbroglio, with his Favourite Consort, and Daniel O'Connell, the great Irish agitator.

There was the Glaciarium, off Tottenham Court Road, with a surface of four thousand five hundred square feet of artificial ice, a picturesque glacier, painted scenery and a promenade orchestra. In lecture rooms throughout the city there was a great choice of panoramas and dioramas of topographical views and battle scenes. The Ojibbeway Indians, under their new management, were back in the Egyptian Hall, in the upstairs room lately occupied by the model of Venice.

During Easter week the exhibitions offered a greater variety of attractions than the theatres, which continued to provide the mixture as before. Alfred Bunn's season of opera and ballet still carried on at Drury Lane. "Why do you not produce legitimate drama?" cried the admirers of Macready. "Because the head of taste is rather considerably turned," Bunn retorted. "Heels light as they are or may be, will weigh down any intellect when put into the scale of present public favour." At Covent Garden that other panderer to the public taste, Monsieur Jullien, continued his promenade concerts. The other theatres provided their yearly extravaganza, which was as statutory at Easter as was the panto-mime at Christmas.

At the Theatre Royal, Haymarket, it was *The Drama at Home*, by James Robinson Planché, who took as his theme the present state of the theatre, the Spirit of Drama visiting all the theatres in London, to seek in vain for a resting place. The grand finale was a procession of the London exhibitions:

Puff: Will you receive the London Exhibitions?
Drama: Yes, for I'm told there are such sights to see
The town has scarcely time to think of me.

Actors impersonating the Exhibitions now entered in proces-sion, preceded by Banner-bearers and Boardmen. The first to advance were the Ojibbeway Indians singing:

The names of two great warriors whom you here may see
Are Pat-au-ah-gust-ah-we-be and Gish-e-gosh-e-ghe.
And after such a specimen of Ojibbeway,
I presume you'll excuse me at once if I say—
Ojibbeway—jibbeway Indians!
Ojibbeway—jibbeway O!

They were followed by Tom Thumb singing,

Yankee Doodle went to town,
On a little pony
This little man of great renown,
Who struts like little Boney.

Next came Madame Tussaud with Commissioner Lin on one arm and his Favourite Consort on the other.

To see you in clover comes Madame Tussaud,
Your model in wax-work she wishes to show,
The King of the French and Fieschi the traitor,
Commissioner Lin and the Great Agitator,
Kings, Princes, and Ministers all of them go,
To sit for their portraits to Madame Tussaud.

Next came the Diver and the Diving Bell.

Oh don't he look a love,
In his helmet and coatee
Rendered waterproof to rove
In the deep deep sea!
Than the wave he dives below
He can cut a greater swell
And to match this diving Beau,
Here behold a diving Bell.
For a shilling if you please,
You inside may take a seat,
And an ocean sound at ease
In the midst of Regent Street.

Finally, the Chinese Collection advanced, with the actors and actresses dressed in Chinese costume, and the orchestra struck up the Chinese Dance, a catchy tune that was to be played, sung and whistled everywhere for the next few weeks.

Ching-a-ring-a-ring-ching! Feast of Lanterns!
What a crop of chop-sticks, hongs and gongs!
Hundred thousand Chinese crinkum-crankums,
Hung among the bells and ding-dongs!

Madame Tussaud danced with Commissioner Lin, and Tom Thumb with the Favourite Consort.

What a lot of Pekin pots and pipkins,
Mandarins with pig-tails, rings and strings,
Funny little slop-shops, cases, places,
Stuck about with cups and tea things!

The Ojibbeways danced with the Diver and the Diving Bell, and all the cast joined in.

> *Women with their ten toes tight tucked into*
> *Tiddle-toddle shoes one scarcely sees;*
> *How they all got here is quite a wonder!*
> *China must be broken to pieces!*

Barnum's delight at the publicity he was getting for Tom Thumb in *The Drama at Home* was somewhat modified when he realised that there were many people, editors of newspapers among them, who were under the impression that it was Tom Thumb himself who was performing in the extravaganza. This was a misapprehension that must be corrected without delay, so he inserted an advertisement in all the newspapers stating that the child who impersonated the General in the extravaganza was only three years old and more than a head taller, as had been fully demonstrated by standing them side by side. The situation worked to Barnum's advantage, for many of those who had seen the child impersonating Tom Thumb at the Haymarket Theatre now wanted to compare him with the genuine article at the Egyptian Hall, with the result that more people than ever came to see Tom Thumb.

Throughout May Barnum continued to exhibit Tom Thumb at the Egyptian Hall before capacity audiences. The great room, still filled with Catlin's Indian Collection, provided a colourful and bizarre setting for the dwarf. The desire of the public to see the dwarf who had so taken the fancy of the Queen was intensified by Barnum's advertisements, which all announced the imminent departure of Tom Thumb for Paris. These advertisements kept the public in a constant state of uncertainty, and caused a rush of visitors to the exhibition, convinced that only a few more days remained for them to see Tom Thumb.

Barnum introduced every performance by pointing out the

presents from the Queen, which were displayed in the room. Tom Thumb then stepped out on to a table, a tiny, elegant figure dressed in a sailor costume. Knowing how he had been received at the Palace, the audience stared at him as though he were something royal and precious. He began his programme with a song, "A Life on the Ocean Wave", and danced a hornpipe. He appeared as a foxhunting man in red coat, breeches and top boots with feet only three inches long. Dressed in full Highland costume, he danced a fling. He impersonated Frederick the Great and Napoleon. He bent his little body to a series of imitations of "Ancient Statues"—the Fighting Gladiator, the Discobulus, the Slave Whetting his Knife, Ajax, Cincinnatus, Samson Carrying the Gates of Gaza, Hercules and the Nemean Lion. His body was so perfectly formed that the audience lost all idea of his diminutive size, and many people remarked on the strange sensation they experienced in his presence: that they were dwarfs and he a person of normal size. The perfection of Tom Thumb's naked little body was best seen when he appeared as Cupid, with bow and quiver, and shot tiny arrows at the ladies in the audience.

As a finale, Tom Thumb appeared in the court suit he had worn before the Queen, and sang this song to the tune of "Yankee Doodle":

> *I'm General Thumb just come to town,*
> *Yankee Doodle Dandy,*
> *I've paid a visit to the Crown,*
> *Dressed like any grandee:*
> *The Queen has made me presents rare;*
> *Court Ladies did salute me;*
> *First rate I am, they all declare,*
> *And all my dresses suit me.*

In the second verse he told of his romps with the Prince of Wales, and in the third and final verse of the great kindness shown to him by Prince Albert:

He loves the Queen, and so do I—
They both say I'm a beauty:
I'm much obliged to all—good bye—
Today I've done my duty.

Besides the three public exhibitions each day, the dwarf performed at private parties for a fee of ten guineas. The demand for his services was so great that frequently he would visit two parties in the same evening. Barnum believed that not a single member of the aristocracy failed to see Tom Thumb either at their own houses, the house of a friend or at the Egyptian Hall. Now that Tom Thumb was well launched in society, Barnum and the dwarf no longer occupied the mansion in Grafton Street. They had found homely lodgings near the Egyptian Hall.

Tom Thumb was now the pet of some of the greatest persons in the land, among them the Dowager Queen Adelaide, the Duke of Buckingham, the Duke of Bedford and the Duke of Devonshire. When the King of Saxony visited Queen Victoria in June an interview with Tom Thumb was one of his first engagements. The Duke of Wellington came several times to the exhibition. The first time he called, Tom Thumb was impersonating Napoleon musing at St. Helena. As the dwarf paced up and down the table, his sombre face deep in meditation, the Duke enquired the subject of his thoughts. "I was thinking of the loss of the battle of Waterloo," the dwarf replied. Barnum saw to it that this ready display of wit was chronicled in every newspaper throughout the country, and he reckoned it was worth thousands of pounds to his exhibition.

Since Easter Tom Thumb had been the most popular attraction in London, but on 5 June he had to take a back seat, for no show, not even Tom Thumb, could compete with the Military Review held in honour of the Emperor of Russia and the King of Saxony at Windsor Great Park. Barnum always regretted that Tom Thumb had not been introduced to the Emperor of Russia, for this was the one omission that marred the brilliance of the dwarf's social achievement in London. Moreover, to Barnum's chagrin, it was such an important omission, for the Emperor was the most illustrious visitor London had had for some time. He had caught the imagination of the public because of the vast extent of his autocratic power over millions of people. It was also considered a democratic touch that so great a ruler should sleep on a sack of straw like the poorest of his subjects. They were not to know that he slept in this manner because he believed it to be conducive not to the good of his soul but to the good of his health.

From early morning on the day of the Review great crowds made their way to Paddington Station. There was hardly a vehicle remaining in London. Every omnibus was crowded and heading out of town. There was not a cab to be found upon the stands. The road to Windsor was an uninterrupted line of carriages and pedestrians. Barnum was among the crowds, for he was the last man to miss a show.

When the royal party arrived at Windsor Great Park they were given a tremendous reception. The Emperor of Russia preceded the Queen's carriage, with Prince Albert on his left and the King of Saxony on his right, the three of them mounted on splendid horses. Next came the Duke of Wellington surrounded by noblemen and officers, Sir Robert Peel among them, his blue frockcoat and buff waistcoat contrasting strikingly with the gorgeous uniforms around him.

As the regiments marched past the royal stand their flags— some bearing the famous names of Corunna and Waterloo— were lowered in salute. On the approach of the Grenadier Guards the Duke of Wellington rode over to them and put himself at the head of his regiment. At this sight there was a roar of cheers from the public for their greatest hero and his men. Barnum, too, was moved by a deep emotion as, in his mind's eye, he saw the whole gorgeous procession marching down Broadway, advertising his American Museum.

The military manoeuvres now got under way. The Artillery brought up their guns and dispersed imaginary squadrons. The Lancers pricked about the ground until they fancied they discovered an enemy, at which they dashed ferociously. The Guards re-enacted their crowning charge at Waterloo, while the Infantry fired volley after volley into them. Barnum marvelled at the precision and rapidity of the foot soldiers. Now they were broken up in divisions; now they formed an impenetrable square; now they were a line as far as the eye could reach, bearing down upon the crowd, which began to retreat before them, until, at the word of command, the whole line was arrested as by an electric shock, and stood before them like a living wall, fixed and immovable.

Barnum reckoned this to be the finest show he had ever seen. The whole dazzling scene, from the Emperor of Russia down to the youngest private in the army, had been beautifully stage-managed by past masters in the art of giving the public what they wanted. He could not have arranged it better himself.

Throughout June the crowds that came to see Tom Thumb showed no signs of slackening off. As in May, Barnum kept the interest of the public in the dwarf at fever pitch by announcing each week that the exhibition was soon to close. To explain why Tom Thumb continued to remain at the Egyptian Hall, these announcements were always followed by others granting an extension of the exhibition because of "the constantly increasing crowds of nobility which attend", and also because of the "numerous requests" from those people who had already seen the dwarf, but wanted the chance to pay him another visit. There were, indeed, many who came to see Tom Thumb again and again.

At the beginning of July interest in Tom Thumb began to wane, so Barnum decided to let the exhibition run for another three weeks and then close it on Saturday, 20 July. This was a convenient date, for on that day the lease of "the great room" he had taken over from George Catlin expired. Even if Barnum had wanted to retain the room for a further period, he could not have done so, for Catlin had renewed the lease for another three months on his own behalf. Fourteen Ioway Indians had arrived in London, and he intended to exhibit them in the room, which still housed his Indian Collection.

Barnum planned a tour of Britain, to be followed by a visit to Paris. But London had not seen the last of Tom Thumb. He was to return to even greater triumphs at the Egyptian Hall. The London public were to lose their wits over him to such an extent that it was almost as though some strange madness had gripped the city. This was how it seemed to Benjamin Robert Haydon, the historical painter, who found himself competing with Tom Thumb for the support of the public; a macabre competition that was to end for Haydon in humiliation, despair and a violent death.

Chapter Six

GENERAL TOM THUMB v.
BENJAMIN ROBERT HAYDON

BENJAMIN ROBERT HAYDON first became aware of Tom Thumb when he read the newspaper account of the Duke of Wellington's visit to the Egyptian Hall to see the dwarf's impersonation of Napoleon musing at St. Helena.

Napoleon was one of Haydon's idols, and to read that he was being impersonated by a dwarf made him feel uneasy. Napoleon was the favourite subject of his paintings. That very morning he had put the finishing touches to his painting of Napoleon in Egypt, musing on the pyramids at sunrise. He never tired of painting Napoleon. He had painted him in many attitudes—musing on the sleeping king of Rome; meditating at Marengo; in his bedroom the night before his abdication; and contemplating his future grave. His favourite study was Napoleon musing at St. Helena. He had painted this thirteen times. He loved to wonder what great thoughts Napoleon was thinking as he stood on the cliffs at St. Helena looking out to the empty sea—this hero, this mysterious being, this Apollyon of the Revelation, this genius, who had fought his way from the school at Brienne until he snatched the crown from the hands of the Pope and put it on his own head: dethroned and exiled, the glory blasted and the pride withered—what great thoughts? Now Haydon read that the Giant Emperor in exile was the subject for an impersonation by a dwarf. Napoleon and Tom Thumb! To Haydon this was a grotesque and blasphemous conjunction. The news item disturbed him deeply. Perhaps, at this moment, he had a premonition of his own fatal link with Tom Thumb, for he cut the paragraph out of the newspaper and wrote in the margin, "I do not like this."

Haydon, like Napoleon, believed himself to be a man of destiny, chosen to accomplish great things. "I am of the Napoleon species," he wrote in his diary. He had dedicated his life to High Art, by which he meant historical painting, the depicting of heroic events on a grand scale. He asserted that the painting of such pictures was the most exalted task an artist could set himself. But historical painting had been out of fashion since the beginning of the century. People preferred to decorate their homes with small pictures of cosy anecdotal subjects. There was no demand for Haydon's enormous canvases, and as he consistently refused to paint anything else, he was always in financial difficulties. No man lived more temperately or worked harder than Haydon, yet in the past twenty-five years he had been arrested for debt seven times, and on four of those occasions he had been sent to prison.

Haydon's financial problems were caused by his habit of borrowing money. He had no shame in borrowing. He believed that the State should support him, because one day his paintings would be the glory of Britain. As the State did not support him, he borrowed money wherever he could. None of his friends was spared. He rarely repaid a debt unless compelled, and then only borrowed the money from someone else. In his early days he had had no difficulty in borrowing. Then he had been regarded as a genius about to startle the world with some great work, and wealthy patrons were willing to lend him money they were not likely to see again. During the six years he devoted to painting *Christ's Triumphant Entry into Jerusalem* he borrowed at the rate of six hundred pounds a year. During these years he was sometimes asked to paint portraits that would have brought him in sufficient money to carry on with his major work without needing to borrow, but he always refused, believing such subjects to be beneath his dignity. Never for a moment would he allow anything to deflect him from his aim—the painting of great pictures.

From boyhood Haydon was diseased with vanity and ambition. In 1804, when he first arrived in London from Plymouth, a student of eighteen, he had fallen down on his knees that night and prayed to be a great painter, to bring honour to his country and to rescue British art from the low state into which he believed it had fallen. Since that night he had never doubted that his mission was to revive the art of historical painting and to establish a national school that would take its place with the greatest in Europe.

At first he had no difficulty in finding patrons. His tremendous confidence, his enthusiasm and his romantic good looks persuaded many influential people that he was a man to watch. He knew all the leading statesmen, writers and artists. Wordsworth and Keats addressed sonnets to him. Many believed, as he did, that one day he would paint a great work that would bring honour to his country. He often spoke of his "day of glory" that was to come, when his name would rank with Michelangelo and Raphael, and buildings decorated with his frescoes would be places of pilgrimage.

In his young days Haydon had painted three huge canvases that were highly praised, *The Judgement of Solomon*, *Christ's Triumphant Entry into Jerusalem* and *The Raising of Lazarus*. Although he was a competent painter, he was by no means the great artist he believed himself to be. He was handicapped by defective eyesight. When working, he wore glasses so concave as to greatly diminish everything in view. Through these he would study his model and his picture from a distance. He would then go up to the canvas and paint, using the naked eye. He would then take up a mirror and examine the reflection of the picture through two pairs of concave spectacles. Then he would return to the canvas, raise his spectacles and resume painting. This method often resulted in a faulty perspective, and many of the heroic figures in his paintings are made ludicrous by the shortness of their legs. Even when Haydon himself noticed an instance of disproportion, he rarely corrected it, so confident was he of his own genius. He wrote of his brush flying over the canvas as if "face, hands, sky, thought, poetry and expression were hid in the handle". Standing back, he would admire his work. "What magic! what fire! what unerring hand and eye! what fancy! what power! what a gift of God! I bow and am grateful."

It was Haydon's tragedy that, of all the fields open to a man of his abilities, he chose the profession of painting, which fed his vanity, indulged his dreams of glory and finally destroyed him. His other talents did, occasionally, find their outlets. He was a great man for causes. He pleaded for them fervidly and earnestly in articles and speeches. He was the first to petition for schools of design in the provinces and for art education in the universities. He argued that the State should encourage artists by commissioning frescoes for public buildings and monuments for national heroes. He believed that the British public had good taste, which could be educated to appreciate High Art, and he gave many lectures up and down the country. All these were good causes, but they did not benefit by having Haydon as their champion. He was too egotistical and vehement. He imputed base motives to anyone who happened to disagree with him. He made powerful enemies, among them Prince Albert and the Royal Academy.

One of the causes he had advocated—the commissioning by the Government of frescoes to decorate public buildings—was implemented in 1842. The Houses of Parliament had been destroyed by fire, and a Royal Commission, presided over by Prince Albert, invited artists to submit cartoons of work to be executed in fresco in the new House of Lords. Haydon had every reason to be confident of winning at least one of the prizes. Not only had he been the first man to suggest this kind of competition but he had also submitted cartoons for frescoes for the old House of Lords as far back as 1812, and laid them before every Prime Minister in succession down to Sir Robert Peel. Moreover, he had long been the solitary champion of historical painting and of these heroic themes for which the Royal Commission was now asking.

The results of the Cartoon Contest were announced on 27 June, 1843, but Haydon was not among the prizewinners. The rejection of his work was a terrible blow to his pride. He felt degraded and insulted. He believed himself to be ill-used. It seemed that authority had decided that he should not be rewarded. He poured out his complaints in a letter to Elizabeth Barrett. She sympathised with him in his disappointment, but she was unwilling to believe in persecution and treachery. Nor did she believe there was a conspiracy against him. "Prizes and crowns," she reminded him, "have been given since the world began to feeble hands and narrow foreheads—because the strong hand and the broad brow can afford to *wait* while the ignorant learn to measure them—not so much because there is malice in the world, as because there is ignorance . . . When Corinna took the crown from over Pindar's head, all Greece looking on, he was mortified and grieved of course—but he did not upbraid his judges with treachery—and who speaks now of Corinna?"

This wise and beautiful letter brought no consolation to Haydon. He craved for recognition in his own lifetime. He could not live without applause. The Cartoon Contest had brought forth a new wave of historical painters, and he, who should have been the leader of the school, had been rejected. That position must, at all costs, be regained. Night after night he lay awake brooding on the result of the contest. Sometimes he would rise with a candle and go to his studio. "There was something grand," he wrote, "something poetical, something touching, something inspiring, something heroic, something mysterious, something awful, in pacing your quiet painting-room after midnight, with a work lifted up on a gigantic easel, glimmering by the trembling light of a solitary candle, 'when the whole world seemed adverse to desert'. There was something truly poetical in devoting yourself to what the vulgar dared not touch—holding converse with the great Spirit; your heart swelling, your imagination teeming, your being rising." At such times he knew himself.

> *Still to be strenuous for the bright reward*
> *And in the soul admit of no decay,*
> *Brook no continuance of weakmindedness,—*

These glorious words were as inspring now as when Wordsworth had addressed them to him so many years ago. Haydon was convinced that his "day of glory" must surely dawn; only the time and place were hidden from him.

These were revealed to him the following year, on the morning of 24 March, 1844, when he was awoken by a voice—"that sort of audible whisper Socrates, Columbus and Tasso heard"—and the voice said, "Why do you not paint your own six designs for the House on your own foundation, and exhibit them?" Haydon was immediately alert. At last he knew what he must do to achieve glory. He knelt up in bed and prayed, "O God! bless the beginning, progression and conclusion of these six great designs . . . Grant me health of mind and body, vigour, perseverance and undaunted courage; let no difficulty or want obstruct me."

The magnitude of his task was appalling. He was fifty-eight years old, his debts were enormous and now he must devote himself to six huge canvases no one had commissioned and which he had little hope of selling. His wife and family tried to dissuade him. They asked him what money would be coming into the house while he was painting these designs. He replied that the exhibition would bring in money, and until then he would do as he had always done—borrow. He reminded them that he had been successful with exhibitions in the past. In 1820 the exhibition of *Christ's Triumphant Entry into Jerusalem* at the Egyptian Hall had made a profit of thirteen hundred pounds. He had proved then that the British public appreciated High Art, and he would do so again. Haydon believed he held a special place in the hearts of the people. He had always had faith in their good taste. In the exhibition of his designs he would appeal from the Royal Commission to the British public and let them decide who was right.

His family argued that the secret voice could have been a delusion, but their arguments were to him like the cries of the sailors in the storm who had urgued Columbus to turn back. "If this be delusion," Haydon wrote, "so was Columbus' voice in the roaring of the Atlantic! but neither was, and under the blessing of God the *result* shall show it as to myself—but only under his blessing." But the result was to be a tragic one for Haydon. For him there was to be no lessening of the storm, no triumphant landfall, but bitter humiliation at the hands of a dwarf and a horrible death.

For the projected six designs, Haydon chose subjects representing just and unjust forms of government. He began with a picture of *Aristides being Hooted by the Populace*. Aristides, the just man, was a self-portrait. The companion to this was to be *Nero Harping while Rome Burned*. He planned to hold an exhibition as soon as the first two designs were completed, for he was anxious that the public should acknowledge without delay the unjustness of the Royal Commission in not awarding him a prize. By January 1846 "Aristides" was finished and "Nero" far enough advanced for Haydon to set Easter Monday as the date of his exhibition. His family and friends tried to dissuade him. They reminded him that he had lost large sums of money by his recent exhibitions. But Haydon could not be discouraged. On 12 January he booked one of the two upstairs rooms at the Egyptian Hall, the one on the right of the landing. He had hoped to get "the great room", where he had exhibited *Christ's Triumphant Entry into Jerusalem* so successfully twenty-six years earlier, but this was not available. On his return from the Egyptian Hall he wrote in his diary, "Took the room, so the die is cast."

In December 1845 Barnum and Tom Thumb returned to London from Paris to give a series of farewell performances before leaving for New York. The visit to France had been a triumph. Barnum had preceded Tom Thumb to Paris, where he had talked with William Rufus King, American Ambassador to the Court of France, who had assured him that after Tom Thumb's audiences with Queen Victoria there should be no difficulty in presenting the dwarf to King Louis Philippe. In February 1845 Barnum brought Tom Thumb to Paris, and on the day after their arrival he received a command to appear with his dwarf at the Tuileries Palace. At the Palace they were introduced to the King and Queen, Princess Adelaide, the Duchesse d'Orléans and her son, the Comte de Paris. The King was amused by the dwarf, and presented him with an emerald and diamond brooch.

Barnum had a favour to ask of King Louis Philippe. Longchamps Day was coming, the mid-Lent carnival held in the Bois de Boulogne, the most fashionable extravaganza of the year, which was attended by the Royal Family and all the aristocracy. Barnum told the King that he had hurried over to Paris to take part in the celebrations, and asked if Tom Thumb's coach could be allowed to drive in the line reserved for the carriages of the Court and the diplomatic corps. He explained that the tiny coach would be in danger of being crushed unless this permission were granted. The King told Barnum to call on the Prefect of Police, who would issue the necessary permit. Tom Thumb and Barnum then withdrew. The dwarf bowed himself out with as fine a grace as any courtier, and the French Royal Family remarked on his perfect knowledge of court etiquette.

On Longchamps Day Tom Thumb drove down the Champs Elysées in the line of carriages reserved for ambassadors to the Court of France. None of the splendid turnouts attracted more attention than the little coach with liveried coachman and four matching ponies. The crowds shouted, "Vive le Général Tom Pouce!" Barnum had never had such an advertisement, and after Longchamps day, whenever the dwarf's carriage made its appearance on the boulevards people flocked from cafés and shops to see it pass. For four months every performance of Tom Thumb was crowded and all seats were booked eight weeks in advance.

In addition to appearing twice daily at the elegant Salle Musard in the Rue Vivienne, Tom Thumb performed for seventy successive nights at the Théâtre du Vaudeville in *Le Petit Poucet*, a five-act play specially adapted for him from Perrault's fairy tale. "Tom Thumb is all in fashion," the *Journal des Débats* reported. "He is the lady-bird of the season; the ladies are passionately fond of him, for the prettiest of them will eagerly press their lips of roses on the bluff cheeks of our little dwarf, who prides himself on having kissed a million of ladies. And he does not lie—as is the habit of every coxcomb. Someday, he will disappear under a heap of nosegays and sweetmeats." In Paris, as in London, all the ladies wanted to pet and kiss the dwarf. Their questions were more pointed than any he had been asked in London or New York, but he answered them readily. Was it his intention to marry? Certainly. To how many was he betrothed? Eight exactly. Was it true that he was unfaithful? Quite true. How many ladies had he kissed? Upwards of a million.

His smallness was a never-ceasing wonder and topic of conversation. It was said that all the costumes which he took to the Tuileries Palace were packed in a container no bigger than a hatbox; that he had escaped the curiosity of some admirers by hiding inside a lady's muff; that his carriage was housed under Barnum's desk and the horses stabled in the sideboard. A café was named "Tom Pouce", and displayed a life-sized figure of him over the entrance. Figures of Tom Pouce in pottery, chocolate and sugar were sold in the shops. Songs were written about him.

He appeared four times before the French Court. He ended one soirée at the Tuileries by appearing in Highland dress. "This costume is the General's triumph," the *Journal des Débats* declared. "We will not mention a celebrated uniform which he wore in London, and which was amazingly successful with our overseas

B. R. HAYDON, ESQ^R.

The artist Haydon at the time of his first exhibition at the Egyptian Hall

Self-portrait by Haydon at the time of his last exhibition

neighbours. The General Tom Thumb had too much good taste to take this costume to the Tuileries. We hope, then, as he possesses such fine feelings, that while he sojourns in Paris, he will leave it at the bottom of his portmanteau." The costume of Napoleon was never worn by Tom Thumb at any of his public appearances in France, but during his final audience with the Royal Family, which took place at the Palace of St. Cloud, he was commanded by King Louis Philippe to give his famous impersonation of Napoleon musing at St. Helena, and he did this before a delighted, if somewhat shocked, Court.

After spending four months in Paris Barnum and Tom Thumb made a tour of France. From Bordeaux they made a brief detour to Spain, where the dwarf appeared before Queen Isabella and the Spanish Court, then assembled at Pampeluna. The Queen presented Tom Thumb with a gold chain. They attended a bullfight together, sitting side by side in the royal box. From Lille they crossed the border into Belgium, where Tom Thumb received a command to appear before the Royal Family at the palace of Laeken. The Queen of the Belgians had seen Tom Thumb at Buckingham Palace, and now she wanted her husband and children to see him. The dwarf's trip to Europe had been not so much a tour as a royal progress.

The taste of the British Royal Family had been endorsed by the royal families of France, Spain and Belgium, and the advertisements for Tom Thumb's farewell season at the Egyptian Hall, to be held during Christmas week, 1845, announced that he would appear "in all the costumes and performances in which he had the honour of appearing three times before Her Majesty, and all the principal courts of Europe". To the display of gifts from Queen Victoria were now added the emerald and diamond brooch from King Louis Philippe and the gold chain from Queen Isabella. All this greatly enhanced the dwarf's prestige, and when the exhibition opened a great crowd came to welcome him back.

Those who had seen him previously remarked how much a

polished man of the world he had become. Tom Thumb had acquired many social graces during his stay in London, and his European tour had refined him even more. He was now a very sophisticated child. He had always been a precocious one. From the earliest years of his career he was interested in the money he earned. According to Barnum, he was miserly. In January, 1845, when Tom Thumb was eight years old, Barnum made him an equal partner, and although his parents signed the contract, the dwarf never let anyone forget that he was the one who earned the money. Young as he was, Tom Thumb knew that he had sold his body to the public.

Although the audiences at the Egyptian Hall still enjoyed Tom Thumb's repertoire of impersonations, they now preferred to see him as himself, dressed in all the fashion and taste of a dandy. He took out his watch and told them the time, and offered them a pinch of snuff or a cigar, all of which were in scale with his size. His manner was impeccable, but some of the audience were disturbed when they detected him regarding them with a mocking look.

The crowds at the exhibition over the Christmas holiday were enormous, and many people had to be turned away. Barnum would have extended Tom Thumb's season at the Egyptian Hall, but he had already arranged a series of farewell appearances in the provinces, beginning in Newcastle-upon-Tyne on Monday, 29 December. He had then planned to return to America. But now he could not ignore the demands of the London public, and so he booked a room at the Egyptian Hall for a further series of farewell performances to begin on Easter Monday, 1846. He was unable to reserve "the great room" downstairs, because that was not available at Easter, so he booked one of the two smaller rooms upstairs. A few days later the other upstairs room, directly across the landing, was booked by Benjamin Robert Haydon for an exhibition of two of his paintings, also to open on Easter Monday. The scene was now set for the fatal contest between Benjamin

Robert Haydon, historical painter, and General Tom Thumb, the celebrated American dwarf.

During March Haydon was busy with the preparations for his exhibition. As the day approached, the little money he had dwindled to a few shillings, but he managed to raise one hundred pounds to pay the final expenses at the Egyptian Hall. This last hurdle surmounted, he wrote in his diary, "Now, as Napoleon said, I could sleep."

Haydon loved the excitement of exhibitions. The Egyptian Hall had been the scene of his first, when, in 1820, he exhibited his enormous painting, *Christ's Triumphant Entry into Jerusalem*. He was thirty-four years old, and then, as now, much depended on the exhibition. His debts had accumulated at a staggering rate during the six years he had spent on the painting, and he had not a penny to his name. But with feelings of "hope mingled with recklessness", he rented the great room at the Egyptian Hall for a year beginning March 1820. The rent was three hundred pounds, but he had no difficulty in borrowing the money, and he was confident that the exhibition would make a profit.

He had every reason to be confident. Even before the exhibition, *Christ's Triumphant Entry into Jerusalem* was known by reputation. People talked of its colossal size, nineteen feet by sixteen feet, and of the six years spent in the painting. During the previous summer Haydon's studio had been open from two until five in the afternoon, and was visited by "rank, beauty and fashion, by genius and by royalty". Distinguished visitors from abroad came, among them the Grand Duke Michael of Russia, and the artists Canova, Cuvier and Vernet. Everyone declared the painting to be a masterpiece.

When the day came for moving the painting to the Egyptian Hall the great canvas was rolled and carried on the shoulders of three Life Guards, loaned to Haydon by his friend Colonel Barton. At the Hall the painting was framed and hung. The frame weighed six hundred pounds. While hanging the picture, the soldiers and the workmen were nervous. At the first attempt an iron ring, believed to be capable of carrying any weight, snapped like a dry twig. At last the painting was up and the figure of Christ could be seen in all its splendour. As the soldiers and workmen looked upon this pale and awesome representation of their God, they fell silent and took off their caps. Haydon had painted the head of Christ six times before he was happy with it, and even now he did not know if he had been entirely successful. He had tried to combine in the features power and humility, but power had won in the end, and there was no trace of the mildness traditionally associated with Christ's countenance. In the painting could be seen the penitent girl brought to Christ by her mother; the centurion and the Samaritan woman spread their garments on the road; among the vast shouting crowd could be seen Wordsworth's bowed head, Sir Isaac Newton's face of belief and Voltaire's sneer.

The picture was up on the wall, but now all work came to an end, because Haydon had no money to provide the things needed before the exhibition could open—the draperies for decorating the room, the tickets, the invitations to the private day. But he could always command the purse of his patron, Sir George Beaumont, who now sent him a cheque for thirty pounds. The work began again. "Now," Haydon wrote, "with upholsterers, soldiers and journeymen in full work, the picture up and looking gloriously, everybody waiting for the word of command to buy hangings and begin fittings, myself ready to glaze, oil staring me in the face, picture reproaching, the sun shining, my palette set, the landlord peeping in now and then, as if half suspicious, there was a halt." The thirty pounds was spent.

Haydon went to his bankers and told them, "I am going to exhibit a painting which has taken six years to paint." They stared at him. "Six years over a picture!" they exclaimed, and lent him fifty pounds. Haydon went straight to the wholesalers, bought the draperies, all in purple brown, and rushed back to the Egyptian Hall. His "thundering voice put fire into all". Women began to sew, boys cleared away, fittings went up. Then Haydon mounted a ladder, palette in hand, ordered the door to be locked and let fly at the picture with a brush brimming with asphaltum and oil.

His students had written and dispatched eight hundred invitations to the private day, he having previously marked the Court Guide. "All the ministers and their ladies, all the foreign ambassadors, all the bishops, all the beauties in high life, the officers on guard at the palace, all the geniuses in town, and everybody of any note, were invited and came." But the morning of the private day brought reaction and exhaustion. He feared that no one would come, and he stayed away from the Egyptian Hall until three-thirty in the afternoon. As he turned into Piccadilly he glanced anxiously at the hall and saw lines of carriages blocking the street. The foyer was crowded, the air was filled with chatter and gaiety. He pushed his way into the exhibition room.

The room was full. Keats and Hazlitt were in a corner, delightedly discussing the picture. The Persian ambassador and his suite had just entered. No one showed any signs of leaving. At five o'clock the crowd was still as great and enthusiastic. But no one had expressed an opinion about Christ's face, it was so novel and unorthodox. Then Mrs. Siddons entered the room majestically and stood before the picture. The whole room remained silent while she studied the painting. After a few minutes Sir George Beaumont asked her delicately, "How do you like the Christ?" Everyone listened for her reply. In a deep tragic tone, she answered, "It is completely successful." The room again became a babble of noise. Everyone agreed with the opinion of the famous actress. Lady Murray said to Haydon, "Why, you have a complete rout." He returned home overwhelmed with joy.

On the following Monday, when the exhibition was opened to the public, crowds rushed to see the painting, and they kept on coming. Sometimes as many as a thousand people came in a day. The painting was a triumph, and when Haydon closed his exhibition in November he had made a clear profit of thirteen hundred pounds. He had proved what he had always claimed, that the British public cared about High Art. And now, twenty-six years later, he hoped to prove it again. But in 1846 he was sixty years old, and as he noted in his diary, "At sixty, men are not so bold."

Haydon's decline in confidence had begun three years earlier, when he had failed to gain a prize in the Cartoon Contest. Since then he had worked hard on the first two of his six designs— 'Aristides' and 'Nero'—which he hoped would retrieve for him his position as the greatest historical painter in the country. He longed to be recognised as a painter of genius, but no one now believed in him or his day of glory. Tastes had changed. His paintings were no longer admired. His influential patrons were either dead or had deserted him. The British public, in whom he had such faith, cared nothing for him. He had become notorious rather than famous. He saw enemies everywhere, and struck out at them ferociously. As his energy dissipated, his creativeness waned, and this deterioration was reflected in "Aristides" and "Nero". During the past three years, with no money coming in and no friends left from whom he could borrow, he had placed himself in the hands of moneylenders. His debts totalled three thousand pounds. Driven half-demented by his predicament, he clung to the hope of his forthcoming exhibition. Everything— his reputation, his solvency—depended on its success.

Tom Thumb returned to London in March, 1846, after a triumphant tour of the provinces. Before leaving London the previous December Barnum had commissioned his friend, Albert Smith, to make an English adaptation of the play *Le Petit Poucet*, in which Tom Thumb had performed in Paris. The French version was too long for British and American tastes, so

Smith compressed it into a playlet of two acts. He rewrote the play in the style of a burlesque, but, on Barnum's instructions, he omitted topical jokes and allusions. Barnum intended to add this play to the dwarf's repertoire, and to present it not only in Britain but also in America. He also instructed Smith to eliminate any technical difficulties, so that the play could be performed in any theatre or exhibition hall, however large or small.

Albert Smith's version, *Hop o' my Thumb*, contained none of the delicate irony of Perrault's original fairy tale, but merely followed the story of the wood-cutter's tiny son, who rescues his brothers from the ogre's castle and makes off with the seven-league boots. With the exception of Hop himself, none of the parts was of great importance. Tom Thumb was to be the attraction. In the course of the play, everything possible was done to emphasise his smallness. He was found curled up inside a hazel nut; he crept into the boss of a daisy; he emerged from a salt cellar; he was concealed under an umbrella; he sheltered in a bird's nest; he led an army of normal-sized men into battle and, turning coward, ran back between the legs of the soldiers; he jumped out of a pie.

Hop o' my Thumb opened at the Lyceum Theatre on Monday, 16 March. The programme also included a two-act drama, *King or Queen*, translated from the French play *Le Loi Salique*, and a farce entitled *Next Door*. After Tom Thumb's poor reception at the Princess's Theatre two years earlier Barnum would not have thought it likely that he would ever again allow the dwarf to appear in another London theatre. But Tom Thumb was now a sensational attraction wherever he performed, and Barnum was determined to milk the situation for all it was worth. *Hop o' my Thumb* did not start until nine o'clock, for Tom Thumb was to appear at the Lyceum after his three daily performances at the Egyptian Hall.

In *Hop o' my Thumb* the dwarf showed that he possessed more acting ability and gift for comedy than anyone had suspected.

The scene in the dormitory of the ogre's castle, when he exchanged his brother's nightcaps for the golden crowns of the ogre's daughters, was a masterpiece of pantomime, and the sight of his little legs running hastily across the stage when he had completed the deception had the audience roaring with laughter. The last scene showed a bedroom in Hop o' my Thumb's palace, with Lilliputian furniture. The dwarf rose from his bed; a little chamber maid brought him clean linen; he took her round the waist and they danced the polka; a miniature barber shaved him, and left him in the hands of two valets, who dressed him in his general's uniform; and he drove off the stage in his famous blue-and-white carriage drawn by four tiny ponies.

When the curtain fell, Tom Thumb was called for again and again. He was literally covered with bouquets, some of which were taller than he was. The opening night of *Hop o' my Thumb* was the greatest theatrical event of the month. The play was to be performed over two hundred times in Britain. Not to have seen it was considered unfashionable. Even Macready, admittedly "with no relish", fell in with Dickens's suggestion that they should visit the Lyceum to see Tom Thumb.

These nightly performances, in addition to three daily exhibitions at the Egyptian Hall, must have been a punishing routine for a child of nine, but neither the dwarf's mind nor body seemed weighed down by the effort. He was as lively at midnight as he was at noon. Some people who saw him believed he was more than human. An Irish scene shifter at the Lyceum, watching Tom Thumb performing on the stage, remarked uneasily, "If they had a thing like that in my country they would be putting him on a hot shovel over the fire to see would he fly up the chimney." And many others, especially among the audiences in Scotland and Ireland, suspected Tom Thumb to be a changeling or a fairy child.

On 25 March Haydon moved his pictures into the Egyptian Hall. For the next few days he was busy addressing four hundred invitations to the private day. He attached a jocose example of the invitation card to his diary.

PRIVATE DAY

Egyptian Hall, Piccadilly, upstairs to the right

Admit *Noodle, Doodle & their numerous Friends* to the private view of Haydon's Two New Pictures, "The Banishment of Aristides" and "Burning of Rome", part of a series for the Decoration of the old House of Lords.

On Saturday the 4th instant, from 12 till six.

Haydon was still in high spirits on 27 March, when he saw his wife off to Brighton, where she was going for a short holiday. But when driving to the station the cab horse fell. This incident disturbed him. The same thing had happened before the Cartoon Contest. He regarded it as an omen. He remembered that Napoleon's coach had broken down on his return from Elba. Two further incidents occurred that he believed to be bad omens. On 31 March, while posting the invitations to the private day, he let three-quarters of them fall on to the pavement. And on 4 April, the morning of the private day, one of the paintings in the exhibition fell off the wall. He wondered what success could come after this.

No more than half a dozen of those invited came to the private day. Admittedly it was raining, but Haydon knew that twenty-six years ago the weather would not have prevented people from coming. He was bitterly disappointed. For most of the afternoon he sat with his daughter, Mary, in an empty room. "Rank, beauty and fashion" had deserted him, but he clung to the hope that the public would support him when the exhibition opened in Easter Week. His daughter warned him that the public were more likely to seek after curiosities than pay attention to art, but Haydon did not agree. He had always had great faith in the good taste of the British public, and he believed that he held a special place in their hearts. If he appealed to them to support his exhibition they would come in their thousands, as they had come to see *Christ's Triumphant Entry into Jerusalem.*

He did appeal to them in an advertisement that appeared in *The Times* on Saturday, 11 April, and again on Easter Monday, 13 April:

HAYDON'S NEW PICTURES are now OPEN at the Egyptian Hall, upstairs to the right. Admission 1s.; catalogues 6d. In these two magnificent pictures of the Burning of Rome by Nero and Banishment of Aristides "the drawing is grand and characters most felicitous, and we hope the artist will reap the reward he merits," says *The Times*, April 6. "These are Haydon's best works," says the *Herald* same day. N.B. Visitors are requested to go up into the gallery of the room, in order to see the full effect of the flame of the burning city. Nero accused the Christians of this cruel act; covered hundreds of them with combustible materials, and burnt them for the amusement of the savage Romans—(See Tacitus). Haydon has devoted 42 years to improve the taste of the people, and let every Briton who has pluck in his bosom and a shilling in his pocket crowd to his works during Easter week.

"An advertisement of a finer description to catch the *profanum vulgus* could not be written," Haydon said on Easter Monday, "yet not a shilling was added to the receipts." Throughout Easter week it seemed as though every Briton with a shilling in his pocket came to the Egyptian Hall to see Tom Thumb. From the door of his empty exhibition room the shabby and dilapidated figure of Haydon watched the crowds surge past him along the landing. The sight filled him with bitterness.

The public in whom Haydon had trusted had let him down. He was mortified by the knowledge that they would rather watch the antics of a dwarf than look at his finest paintings. He had felt humiliated and degraded after the Cartoon Contest, but this was far worse. Then the Royal Commission had rejected him in favour of other artists, now the public had rejected him in favour of a dwarf. The insult was unbearable, and he struck out savagely at the public in an advertisement that he published in *The Times* on 21 April:

Exquisite Feeling of the English People for High Art—GENERAL TOM THUMB last week received 12,000 people, who paid him £600: B. R. HAYDON, who has devoted 42 years to elevate their taste, was honoured by the visits of 133½, producing £5. 13. 6, being a reward for painting two of his finest works, 'Aristides and Nero'. HORACE VERNET, LA ROCHE, INGRES, CORNELIUS, HESS, SNORR, and SCHEFFER, hasten to this glorious country of fresco and patronage, and grand design, if you have a tender fancy to end your days in a Whig Union. 'Ingenuas didicisse', etc.

This advertisement aroused widespread comment, but did little to further Haydon's cause, for most people were offended by it. The *Art Union* expressed "extreme regret".

If Haydon's advertisement did not achieve much at least it gave *Punch* another opportunity to attack the Royal patronage of Tom Thumb. After warning Haydon that in his comment on Tom Thumb he had shown a great want of respect towards very distinguished persons, *Punch* continued, "In the first place, the 12,000 people who visited Tom Thumb did not visit a mere dwarf . . . no, it was to pay a reverence to one whom royalty delights to honour. Tom Thumb is not to be considered as a dwarf, but as an abstraction of highest taste. Has he not had rings and watches given him by Queens, and pencil-cases by Princes and Dukes? Is he not shown as a creature honoured and valued by the great? Very well, Mr. Haydon. Let 'High Art' in England obtain the same patronage—let it receive as cordial a welcome at the Palace, as again and again has been vouchsafed to Tom Thumb,— and crowds of snobs, for such only reason, will rush to contemplate it—or to think they contemplate it."

Punch went on to query the 133½ visitors who had, according to Haydon's advertisement, come to see the paintings. "That ½ is touching. What sort of $\frac{1}{2}$ was it? Did it run alone, or being brought to drink in High Art, was it a baby at the breast?" It was, in fact, a little girl.

The British public, whether amused or offended by Haydon's advertisement, could not know the agony of the man who had composed it. Haydon's exhibition, the one that was to justify his claim to be the greatest artist in the country, had failed. All his hopes had been destroyed by a dwarf. And more cruel still, it seemed to Haydon that Tom Thumb, by impersonating with his stunted body the great heroic figures of the past, mocked and degraded the values to which he had dedicated his life. Ajax, Samson, Cincinnatus, Frederick the Great and Napoleon were all subjects worthy of the finest historical art, to be depicted not smaller than life, but larger, much larger. Yet across the landing the impersonations of these illustrious figures by a strutting pigmy were being acclaimed by a demented public, whose shouts affronted the silence of his room as he sat alone beneath his two greatest paintings.

Was it a wonder that he struck out so savagely? After Haydon's frightful death Elizabeth Barrett wrote to Robert Browning, "And could a man suffering *so*, stop to calculate very nicely the consideration due to A, and the delicacy which should be observed towards B? Was he scrupulously to ask himself whether this or that cry of his might not give C a headache? Indeed no, no. It is for *us* to look back and consider! Poor Haydon. As to grief as grief—of course he had no killing grief. But he suffered."

Easter week 1846 was one of Barnum's most successful weeks in London. The public crowded to the Egyptian Hall believing that this would be their last chance to see Tom Thumb before he returned to America. The following week all the performances were again crowded, and many people had to be turned away. Barnum was using his technique of announcing each week as the last week for seeing Tom Thumb, but now he was succeeding too well. The police were objecting to the press of carriages and people that blocked Piccadilly throughout the afternoon and early evening. The attendants at the Egyptian Hall could not control the crowds. People who had bought their tickets in advance were unable to gain admission. The exhibition room was crowded to suffocation, and many people fainted. To bring some measure of control into the situation, Barnum announced that "on account of the unprecedented success and crowded state of the room at each levee, the little general begs respectfully to inform the nobility, gentry and public that he will continue to appear".

One of the most curious manifestations of the exhibition was the attraction Tom Thumb had for women. They grew soft and tender-hearted over him. They looked upon him sometimes as a man and sometimes as a child. They wanted to kiss and caress him. These were strange sensations for Victorian ladies, but ones they shared with those ladies of ancient Rome who liked to have dwarfs running about their apartments, naked and bedecked with jewels.

At every performance the women outnumbered the men by ten to one. Their ribbons and summer dresses made the exhibition room bright with colour. When Tom Thumb stepped on to the table they shrieked with delight. They called him precious names —Darling, Duck, Cherub, Angel—while he stood there like a peacock. He addressed some of his songs especially to them. He could move them to tears when he sang,

> *I should like to marry, if I could only find*
> *Any pretty lady suited to my mind.*

As they listened, at least one member of the audience wondered whether Queen Victoria would find Tom Thumb a bride as Queen Henrietta had found a tiny husband for her court dwarf, Anne Shepherd, and whether Prince Albert would give the bride away as Charles I had done.

Then Tom Thumb's mood would change from sentimental to saucy as he skipped about the table singing,

I am a very little man, my name is Tommy Thumb,
I always kiss the ladies, when to see me they do come.

And many ladies were kissed by him, for at the end of each performance he sold kisses, together with the pamphlet account of his life, for one shilling. Those who had been kissed usually wanted to kiss him back, and so many kisses were implanted on his cheeks that every night he had to soothe them with cold cream and rosewater. Some ladies picked him up and fondled him, but he always struggled against this indiginity, for he had been carefully schooled by Barnum to behave like an adult and never to respond, as a child might naturally do, to the tenderness of a woman. "You hippopotamuses!"—so *Punch*, in a Yankee accent, derided these ladies—"haven't you got nothing of your own at home to nurse—no babbies; or, if no babbies, not even a spaniel or a kitten, to make a screeching hubbaboo about, but you must come out o' your own houses, to break your stay-laces, and have your ribbons—that cost them honest critters, your husbands, so much—tore slick off your bonnets, scrouging to see the smallest piece on airth of human natur?"

Once again Barnum was indebted to *Punch* for serving up the General "so daintily". Far from shaming the ladies, the publicity encouraged those who had not seen the dwarf to visit the exhibition.

Involved in debts beyond the hope of paying, Haydon's mind oscillated between hope and despair. He knew his financial position to be one of extreme peril because of the failure of the exhibition, yet when he awoke on the morning of 16 April, his mind was filled with ideas for the next painting in his series, *King Alfred and the First English Jury*. Mortified by the lack of public support for the first two paintings, he wondered, "Is this the whisper of an evil or of a good spirit?" But he believed it must be that of a good spirit, and falling on his knees, he asked for God's blessing on this painting. "I call on him who has led me through the wilderness for forty-two years, under every depression and every excitement, not to desert me in this the 11th hour."

Haydon began working on his new painting, stimulated, if anything, by his troubles. "How mysterious," he mused, "is the whisper which in such anxieties impels to paint, conceive and invent. How mysterious!" Against the advice of his family, he kept the exhibition open, and he borrowed money to pay the wages of the attendants at the Egyptian Hall. "No man," he claimed, "can accuse me of shewing less energy, less spirit, less genius than I did twenty-six years ago. I have not decayed, but the people have been corrupted. I am the same, they are not, and I have suffered in consequence." During these days he often thought of Napoleon. "I used to accuse Napoleon for want of energy in not driving out the Senate, as he did on 18 Brumaire (9 November, 1799), after Waterloo, but he knew men better than me—he knew it would have been useless; *he* was not altered, *they* were."

As the month of May began, Haydon wrote in his diary, "My dangers are great." The number of debts due for repayment was increasing, and his wife and family awaited each day with fear. "Money fled, the butcher, the baker, the tax collector, the land-lord give louder knocks than before." The exhibition, on which he had pinned all his hopes, was bringing nothing in. On 4 May his affairs reached a crisis. The morning post brought a lawyer's letter demanding repayment of a client's loan and a bill from the proprietor of the Egyptian Hall for thirty pounds for rent unpaid. He spent a fruitless day trying to raise money, but the best he could do was to persuade the lawyer to give him more time. Oppressed as he was by financial worries, as he sat waiting in the lawyer's chambers, the whole background of his new painting flashed through his mind, and he hurried home, "in sorrow, delight, anxiety and anticipation", to set to work. Arriving there, the cook, whose wages he had not been able to pay, handed him a card from a broker saying he had called for a quarter's rent for the landlord.

Haydon went to his studio. He set his palette, but he could not work, for his brain was harassed and confused. He fell into an exhausted sleep, from which he awoke stiff and cold. But he flew at the painting and worked until he had put in the new background. He dined that evening expecting a summons at any moment, and went to bed in misery. The next morning an unexpected cheque arrived from a friend, which enabled him to pay off some of the most urgent debts. "This," Haydon remarked bitterly, "is historical painting in England."

On Monday, 18 May, Haydon closed his exhibition. The following day he cleared his paintings out of the Egyptian Hall. The removal men had to struggle with "Aristides" and "Nero" along a landing and down a staircase crowded with people waiting to see Tom Thumb. Haydon shut the door of the empty room behind him and walked down the stairs. "Next to a victory, is a skilful retreat," he said, "and I marched out before General Thumb, a beaten but not conquered exhibitor."

"The Banishment of Aristides" by Haydon

Cruikshank's etching "John Bull among the Lilliputians"

"I dreamt I slept at Madame Tussaud's"

Chapter Seven

"TOM THUMB FOR EVER!"

THE NUMBER of people wanting to see Tom Thumb showed no signs of lessening, so Barnum extended the farewell season for a further four weeks from Monday, 18 May. Tom Thumb's triumphs in London encouraged other dwarfs to try their luck there. So many came that it seemed as though Britain had become the asylum for all the dwarfs in the world. "For Tom Thumb's successes," *Punch* declared, "successes stamped in imperishable gold—have called forth dwarfs from every nook and corner of the earth. England has taught human nature the exceeding advantage of being little. Hence, we have had German dwarfs—Spanish dwarfs—and, very recently, dwarfs from the Highlands; dwarfs who have danced their national lilts at the Palace to the eternal glory of the Land of Cakes."

The Highland dwarfs were exhibited in the summer of 1846 at the Cosmorama Rooms, Regent Street. They were named Mackinlay and came from the county of Ross. The eldest dwarf, Finlay, was twenty-three years old and forty-five inches high. His brother, John was twenty-one years old and forty-four inches high. His sister, Mary, was nineteen years old and forty-four inches high. In Scotland they had been employed as shepherds, but an Edinburgh showman persuaded them to come to London by telling them of the patronage Tom Thumb was receiving from the Queen. Nor were they disappointed. The Queen's delight in dwarfs, together with her predilection for all things Scottish, assured them of an audience. On 21 May the dwarfs, dressed in the tartan of the clan of Ross, gave a performance of Scottish songs and dances at Buckingham Palace before the Queen, Prince Albert and the Duchess of Kent.

About the same time Richard Garnsey, a dwarf from Somerset, was exhibited at the Gallery of British Artists, Suffolk Street. Garnsey was thirty-three inches high. A certificate of his birth proved him to be fifteen years old. He had been examined by a panel of eminent doctors, presided over by Sir James Clark, the Queen's physician, and pronounced to be "the most symmetrical dwarf in the world". He was billed as the "Miniature John Bull", a title so patriotic that one would have thought it certain to gain him an audience with the Queen, but, for some unknown reason, the royal courtesy was not extended to the loyal little fellow from the West Country. Garnsey's programme of songs and mime pleased his audiences, but the lack of Royal favour put him at a disadvantage with his rivals.

Another dwarf who deserved a better reception was Don Francisco Hidalgo, dwarf to the Court of King Ferdinand VII of Spain. The Don was forty-two years old and twenty-nine inches high, well formed and handsome. For eighteen years he was attached to the Court of Madrid; for twelve years he had been living in retirement. His tastes were intellectual, and he spoke several languages. The reports of an American dwarf exciting the curiosity of London made him decide to come before the public. He wondered what would be the feelings of those who were astonished at the exhibition of a small child on seeing a mature man of intellect and beauty only twenty-nine inches high. In the summer of 1846 Don Francisco Hidalgo came to London, but he was not received by the Queen. The audiences who came to his performances at the Cosmorama Rooms saw a distinguished figure with a small moustache and long hair which fell in a roll over his ears. But the melancholy songs he sang to the accompaniment of his little guitar were not to the taste of a public accustomed to the brashness and vivacity of Tom Thumb, and Don Francisco Hidalgo soon returned to his library and his studies.

Dwarfs came to London from as far away as Africa. Some stunted Bushmen were exhibited under the outlandish title of the Boshie Men. The curious "yuk yukking" sounds they emitted frightened some of the audience. There are no reports that the Boshie Men were kissed and fondled by the ladies, and even the Queen declined to receive them.

The invasion of London by dwarfs was the subject of an etching by George Cruikshank entitled *John Bull among the Lilliputians*, which depicts John Bull spreadeagled on the ground, secured by ropes and stakes. By means of ladders the dwarfs have mounted his stomach. Tom Thumb is stealing his watch. Don Francisco Hidalgo searches for money in one trouser pocket while the Highland dwarfs search in another. The Boshie Men have found his purse. In the distance more dwarfs are approaching. "Dear me!" John Bull says, "how very funny."

The popularity of the dwarfs gave some people cause for concern. There were those who feared that if the public wanted dwarfs every means would be employed to produce them. Demand creates supply, and there was a danger that the unscrupulous parent would become a Prospero to rear a Caliban. Infants would be given gin, a spirit traditionally believed to stunt growth, and their limbs would be squeezed and contorted. These fears were expressed by Angus Bethune Reach in *Douglas Jerrold's Shilling Magazine*, in words addressed to the fathers and mothers of Britain.

"Has it never struck you," Reach asked them, "that by rushing in crowds, as you have done, to see—and pay for the show—a miserable object, a stunted infant, you have been in fact offering a premium with cupidity to unite with nature when she shows herself unkind, in order to produce again a something which shall be world's wonder and an owner's profit? There have been many 'infant phenomena' on the stage and in the booth. The public has patronised these disgraceful, these—one would think, to a pure and natural mind—disgusting exhibitions. Who shall say how many poor infantine limbs have been clogged, how many poor infantine frames have been dosed and drugged to produce like monstrosities. If people will pay largely for the sight of what is unnatural, rest assured that the unnatural, so far as man can make it, will be manufactured for the market."

This point was taken up by *Punch*, which published an imaginary letter from "Nicholas Catchpenny", a poor man anxious to earn a little money. He wanted to know by what means he could check the growth of his two-year-old baby. He had tried gin with no effect, except that of throwing the child into a fever. His object was to make the child into a dwarf in order to exhibit it. "I am told," Catchpenny continued, "that the proprietor of Tom Thumb is making a rapid fortune in this manner, with little or no exertion; and this is just what I want to do too. If you could tell me of any drug, or any system of treatment whereby I might stunt my child's proportions without endangering its life—for, of course, I should be sorry to lose it—you would oblige me."

None of the dwarfs on exhibition in the West End had been artificially stunted; they were all perfectly formed, unlike the misshapen cretins usually exhibited as dwarfs at country fairs. But some people were disgusted at the exhibition of any dwarf, whether symmetrical or not, believing both kinds to be equally diseased. "Do you know what you have been about?" Reach asked the ladies who had kissed Tom Thumb. "Do you know that partial or faulty development is nothing but disease? You would not be amateurs in pathology. You would not flock admiringly around *fungus haemotodes*, or expatiate in raptures on the wonderful merits of a case of rickets. Cancer and crooked limbs are horrible, and you shrink from them. Dwarfishness, ladies, is not less disease, that there is nothing absolutely repulsive in its features. There must be some lack of natural power, of natural health when the body does not become developed. This want might be shown in a thousand hideous ways, in a thousand diseases. Sometimes it manifests itself in dwarfishness—the disease of littleness."

Reach pleaded for a stop to be put to these exhibitions. "Let public opinion confess its error; and in future, when a dwarf is born, let its parents tend with the holiest love the unhappy being thus arriving, a monstrous creature, into the world. Let retirement be the lot of the being whom nature has prevented from mingling freely with its fellow-creatures. Let the brand be covered the stigma hid. Let the secrecy of private dwelling or public asylum enwrap it. Let us have no unfortunates—the victims at once of nature's mysterious displeasure and the world's insolent and heedless curiosity."

But the dwarfs were too lively a race to be thus consigned to obscurity, and, as *Punch* declared, "every little lump of humanity from the shilling's-worth at the Egyptian Hall to the pennyworth at the Greenwich Fair", continued to divert the British public, and to make "the *maximum* profit with the *minimum* material".

The month of June brought one of the longest spells of fine weather for twenty-five years. On Whit Monday, 1 June London baked in a heatwave and holidaymakers sought cool breezes. Railway trips were heavily booked. The trains leaving London stations for the coast were sometimes a quarter of a mile in length. The road to Hampton Court was jammed with carriages. Those who did not travel spent the day in the parks, and every inch of cool green turf was covered with picnickers. Outdoor places of entertainment boomed. Vauxhall Gardens, usually associated with umbrellas and rain, was in carnival mood, and the theme was chinoiserie. Monsieur Tourniaire's equestrian troop, dressed as Chinese cavalry, wound its way over the bridges. A pagoda was the set-piece on the firework ground. Joel Il Diavolo dived one hundred and twenty feet astride a dragon belching fire.

The traditional Whit Monday Fair was held at Greenwich, and from dawn until sunset there was uproar on the Thames. Steamboats carried thousands up and down the river, and some of the boats were so overloaded that at every roll the water washed in through the cabin windows. The Fair was held in a cul-de-sac below the church. The interiors of the side-shows were like ovens. The Learned Birds, half a dozen dirty canaries, huddled dispiritedly on their perch. In the Wild Animal show a disconsolate trainer, in the tattered uniform of a Roman gladiator, kept guard over a mangy ostrich and tiger, which panted with thirst in the dusty heat.

The theatres were half-empty, but despite the heatwave, Tom Thumb had record attendances at his Whitsun performances. During Whit week the weather was intensely hot. At one time the temperature in the sun was 126 degrees, and on several occasions during the week the thermometer was as high as 95 degrees in the sun and 85 degrees in the shade. The temperature continued to remain high during the following week. The hot weather made bathing popular. In the course of eight days the number of bathers in the Serpentine was no less than sixty-five thousand. The healthiness of the weather was remarked upon. The number of deaths was much below the average for the month.

Haydon began the month of June "in fear and submission". His financial position was desperate because of the failure of his exhibition. He remarked bitterly how his former pupil, Edwin Landseer, painter of sentimental animal pictures, had already earned that year nearly seven thousand pounds, while he had been forced to withdraw two of his finest historical paintings at a loss. These paintings now lay in a corner of his studio. "Aristides, unasked for, unfelt for, rolled up, and Nero—Aristides, a subject Raphael would have praised and complimented me on. Good God!—and £111-8-10 loss for showing it." His total debts were in excess of three thousand pounds, and some of the most pressing ones were due that month. He had £15 to pay on the 12th, £17 10s. 6d. on the 14th, £26 10s. on the 24th, two repayments of £31 17s. 6d. and £30 on the 25th, and one of £29 16s. 9d. on the 29th. A total of £135 14s. 9d., and only 18s. in the house. The entry in his diary for 11 June reads, "Nothing

coming in, all received, no orders of any description, one large
picture painting, and three more getting ready, and Alfred's
head to do. In God alone I trust, in humility. Amen."

Haydon's days were divided between working at his painting
of King Alfred and walking in the City in a fruitless quest to raise
money and to buy time. The heat made him irritable. The pave-
ments were hot even through the soles of his boots. Business details harassed and confused him, but when he arrived home he
could always find solace in his work. "When I paint," he wrote,
"I feel as if nectar was floating in the interstices of the brain." The
desire to finish the remaining pictures in his great series obsessed
him, and each day he prayed that nothing on earth would stop
their completion. On 13 June a friend who had promised to lend
him one thousand pounds told him that he was unable to fulfil his
promise. After hearing this news Haydon did something he had
never done before, he got drunk. For the next few days he was
deeply agitated. His mind was confused. He could not sleep.
Even the comfort of work was now denied him. He sat in his
studio staring at his painting like an idiot. His wife and family
were frantic with anxiety. They noticed that his face was flushed
and haggard and that he kept pressing his hand to his head. On
16 June he told them of the gravity of his position. Later in the
day he went to the pawnshop with the household silver to raise a
little ready money in case of an emergency. On 18 June he wrote
to Elizabeth Barrett asking if she would give shelter at her home
in Wimpole Street to five pictures and three trunks containing
his private papers, which he wished to safeguard from his credi-
tors. One of the trunks contained the twenty five volumes of his
diary—all but the current one.

London was gayer in the hot weather. Mignonette flowered in
the window boxes, balconies were shaded by brightly striped
awnings and pianos sounded through the open doors in quiet
streets. The weather was perfect for promenading in Kensington
Gardens and Regent's Park. Ladies wore the lightest of summer

dresses and protected themselves from the sun with parasols of watered silk. Gentlemen wore transparent gauze waistcoats and blouse-like paletots. Iced sherry cobbler was the favourite drink. Boys clustered round Wenham Lake Ice Depots as if the mere sight of the large blocks of ice would cool them, and the diver who passed the greater portion of his life at the bottom of the tank at the Polytechnic Institute aroused envy.

Few people thought of going to the theatre. At no time were the theatres more than half-full, and plays had to be taken off through lack of support. By the middle of the month managers were declaring that the theatre had never done so badly in living memory. On the other hand, the lovely weather was making the fortunes of proprietors of alfresco resorts. Vauxhall Gardens, Cremorne Gardens and Surrey Gardens were crowded every evening. Londoners standing on the bridges over the Thames could see balloons and fireworks going up in all directions, while below them steamboats, crowded with passengers, cut their way up and down the river. "The masses," the *Illustrated London News* remarked, "are all for out-of-door revelry." The fine weather, however, did not prevent people from coming to see Tom Thumb during the last two weeks of his farewell season at the Egyptian Hall, and at every performance the exhibition room was a sea of moving fans.

The entry in Haydon's diary for 21 June was brief: "Sunday. Slept horribly. Prayed in sorrow and got up in agitation." He told his son, Frank, that, when lying awake, he had understood how it was people committed suicide. In the evening he walked with Frank to Hampstead. In Regent's Park he complained of the heat and held his head as if it hurt him. He became excited. He told Frank it would give him pleasure to throw himself off the Monument and dash his head to pieces. Frank begged him not to think such thoughts, and after a while he became calm.

Haydon rose early the next morning. He went to his studio

THE MODERN GULL IVER.

Illustrations depicting Tom Thumb in London from the
Comic Almanack 1847

NAPOLEON'S ADIEU D'EGYPTIAN HALL.

BORN A GENIUS

Cruikshank's etchings contrasting

BORN A DWARF.

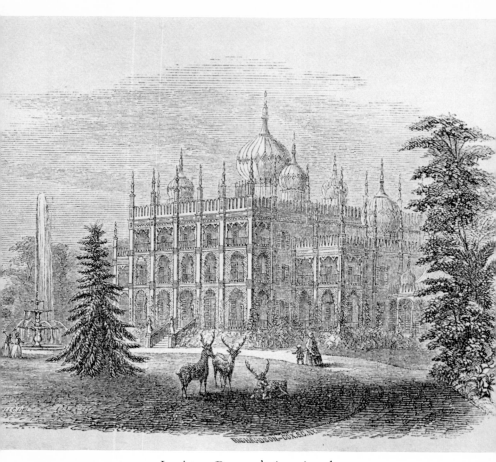

Iranistan, Barnum's American home

and wrote letters until eight-thirty. Then he went out to Oxford Street and bought a pistol from Riviere, the gunsmith. He returned home and locked himself in his studio, where he wrote his will and a number of farewell letters. While he was doing this his wife passed the studio on her way upstairs. She tried the locked door. He spoke sharply to her, and she went away. Shortly afterwards he followed her upstairs and apologised for having spoken so roughly. He kissed her tenderly and returned to his studio, again locking the door.

He then sat down and wrote "The Last Thoughts of B. R. Haydon". As always, Napoleon was in his mind, but now he wondered if the influence of the Emperor had been altogether a good one. "I fear the glitter of his genius rather dazzled me," he wrote. In this last hour he realised what sufferings his vanity had brought on his wife and family, and he begged their pardon, knowing they would now be happier "released from the burden of my ambition".

He finished writing at a quarter to eleven and unlocked the door. Then he put the pistol to his head and pulled the trigger. Death did not follow, for the bullet was deflected by his skull. Although dreadfully wounded, he managed to reload the pistol, then, changing his mind, he dropped it to the floor and seized a razor. He hacked at his throat, making two terrible gashes. He staggered about the room and fell dead before the picture of Alfred, splashing the canvas with his blood.

On a table near the painting he had placed the last volume of his diary, open at the final entry.

God forgive—me—Amen.
Finis
of
B. R. Haydon.
"Stretch me no longer on this tough world"—Lear
End
XXVI Volume.

Mary Haydon, the twenty-two-year-old daughter of the artist, was the first to find the body. Knowing her father to be in low spirits, she had gone to the studio to console him. She entered the room gently so as not to disturb him. At first the room seemed empty. There was an awful silence broken only by the ticking of a watch which lay on a table. Her spirits sank. She felt as if some sorrow had passed into the air. She thought her father was not there, and then she saw him lying on the floor, his head resting upon his right arm. She thought he was studying the foreground of his painting. She called softly to him, but he did not answer. She stepped closer, and her foot slipped in what she thought was a pool of red paint. Then she saw the greenish white face and the terrible wounds across his throat, and she knew she was standing in her father's blood. Mary never recovered from the shock of finding her dead father, and she did not survive him by many years.

When the doctor came he ordered the body to be left undisturbed until the coroner had seen it. That night a great thunderstorm broke over London and dispelled the fierce heat. The storm was accompanied by torrential rain. Lightning flashed in the east and illuminated, through the half-closed shutters, the body of an historical painter, lying on the floor in front of a colossal painting, the third in an unfinished series.

On Monday 22 June, as Haydon lay dead, Tom Thumb began the final week of his farewell season at the Egyptian Hall. In addition to his usual performance, the dwarf sang two songs.

> *Farewell to Albion, where I've been*
> *Three times in state to see the Queen . . .*

And he concluded his performance with the song "Then You'll Remember Me".

When other lips and other hearts
Their tale of love shall tell,
In language where excess imparts
The powers they feel so well;
There may, perhaps, in such a scene,
Some recollection be,
Of days that have as happy been—
Then you'll remember me.

This song, so sweetly sung, moved his audience deeply, and many of the cheeks he kissed afterwards were wet with tears.

The inquest on Benjamin Robert Haydon was held on Wednesday, 24 June, at the Norfolk Arms Tavern, Burford Place, three doors from Haydon's house. After being sworn, the jury went to view the body. Stretched on the floor in front of a picture of *Alfred the Great and the First British Jury*, the latest British jury saw the corpse of an old man, his white hair clotted with blood. He was neatly dressed, and the scene of his death had been arranged with care. A portrait of his wife stood on a small easel immediately facing his large picture. On an adjoining table he had placed the last volume of his diary open at the final entry, some farewell letters, a sheet of paper headed "Last Thoughts of B. R. Haydon", a watch and a prayer book open at the Gospel for the Sixth Sunday after the Epiphany, "For there shall arise false Christs and false prophets, and shall show great signs and wonders; insomuch that (if it were possible) they shall deceive the very elect."

The jury returned to the tavern, where the coroner produced a large folio manuscript volume, the last diary of Haydon. He asked the Reverend Orlando Hyman, a stepson of Haydon, to mark such passages as might throw some light on the state of his stepfather's mind. These passages Mr. Hyman would read to the jury.

After a short interval Mr. Hyman said he was prepared for the task. He had thought it better to go back to the month of April, when his stepfather had been deeply affected by the failure of the exhibition of his paintings at the Egyptian Hall, an exhibition on which he had built his hopes. Mr. Hyman read out Haydon's account of the fatal competition from Tom Thumb.

"April 13. Receipts £1.3.6. They rush by thousands to see Tom Thumb. They push, they fight, they scream, they faint, they cry help and murder, and oh and ah. They see my bills, my boards, my caravans, and don't read them. Their eyes are open, but their sense is shut. It is an insanity, a rabies, a madness, a furor, a dream. I would not have believed it of the English people." "My situation is now one of extreme peril." "April 21. Tom Thumb had 12,000 last week: B. R. Haydon 133½." "May 4. My brain harrassed and confused." "May 18. I have closed my exhibition with a loss of £111. 8. 10." "June 13. My necessities are dreadful owing to the failure of my exhibition at the Hall." "June 15. Passed in great anxiety." "June 21. Slept horribly. Prayed in sorrow and got up in agitation." "June 22. God forgive—me—Amen. Finis of B. R. Haydon."

The jury was unanimous in their verdict. They found that the deceased, Benjamin Robert Haydon, died of the effects of wounds inflicted by himself, and that he was in an unsound state of mind when he committed the act.

All the leading London newspapers published three-column verbatim reports of the inquest, and of all the sensational aspects of Haydon's death the one that struck the public most was the victory of Tom Thumb. It was to be referred to again and again in editorials and cartoons. *The Times* of 26 June made it the subject of a leading article: "The display of a disgusting dwarf attracted hordes of gaping idiots, who poured into the pockets of a Yankee showman a stream of wealth one tithe of which would have redeemed an honourable English artist from wretchedness and death. It is terrible to think, that in the London 'season' of this century, in the heart of the greatest city, and under the eyes of the wealthiest people in the world, such should have been the lot of a gentleman who, if he wanted those pliant qualities which sometimes supersede both talent and merit in wordly success, had almost merit and talent enough to compensate the deficiency, and failed in no other of the requisites for competence and fame. These are the events which compel even sober-minded men towards the conviction that this condition of society should no longer exist, whatever be the cost of the change."

This leading article made a great impression, as did two etchings by George Cruikshank that appeared in the *Comic Almanack*. One picture entitled "Born a Genius" depicts a shabby artist sitting in an attitude of despair in front of an unfinished painting. The other entitled "Born a Dwarf" depicts Tom Thumb in a luxurious room, reclining on a sofa with bags of gold at his feet. The same issue of the *Comic Almanack* contained a fable of a poor woman expecting a baby who asks Jupiter to make her child the richest and happiest of men. Jupiter decides to grant her prayer, and the woman gives birth to a dwarf. The woman, perplexed and sad, tells Jupiter that she had expected the child to be given a mind of genius. The god rebukes her, saying that had he conferred genius the child would have felt only want and neglect in the world. "See how thou wouldst have beggared thy boy with genius," Jupiter continued. "And now listen how I have enriched him with deformity. He shall go forth a wonder to the staring and senseless world. Monarchs shall smile upon him, and rejoice to gird his neck with precious jewels. He shall be the beloved of matrons, and the fondling of damsels. Crowds shall flock to behold him, heaping his little lap with countless riches and costly gifts. His cars shall be drawn through the public ways in triumph; and he—the stunted dwarf—shall play the Giant Emperor among men. Thank thou, then, the Gods, oh woman, whose bounty has given thee a dwarf, and not a genius for thy child."

As the circumstances of Haydon's death became known, a wave of compassion swept the country. It seemed to many that the greatest painter of his generation had perished frightfully through the neglect of his fellow-countrymen. All criticism of Haydon and his work was stilled. The obituaries were unanimous in their certainty of the high place he would occupy in the history of British art. While people vied with each other in the fulsomeness of their appreciation one man, at least, kept a sense of proportion, and that was Charles Dickens. Dickens was later to combine the less admirable qualities of both Haydon and Leigh Hunt in the character of Harold Skimpole in *Bleak House*. He thought the account of the inquest one of "the most affecting pieces of fact" he had ever heard, nevertheless he believed that Haydon had been utterly mistaken in his vocation. "No amount of sympathy with him," Dickens wrote to a friend, "and sorrow for him in his manly pursuit of the wrong idea for many years—until by dint of perseverance and courage it almost began to seem the right one—ought to prevent one from saying that he most unquestionably was a very bad painter, and his pictures could not be expected to sell or to succeed. I went to that very exhibition at the Egyptian Hall, of which he writes so touchingly in his Diary. And I assure you that when I saw his account of the number of visitors he had had in one of the papers, my amazement was—not that there were so few, but that there were so many. There was one picture, Nero entertaining himself with a musical performance while Rome was burning—quite marvellous in its badness. It was difficult to look at it with a composed and decent face. There is no doubt, on the other hand, that in the theory of his art, he was very clever, and in his general tone of thought a very superior man and I must say that having written so well on art, and having suffered so much in a hopeless attempt to elevate it, I think he was (as his widow is) a very good subject for a pension."

The plight of Haydon's widow became a matter of public concern. On 30 June a meeting was held at the chambers of Serjeant Talfourd, in Serjeant's Inn, to devise measures of providing for Mrs. Haydon and her daughter. Many prominent men attended. The Prime Minister, Sir Robert Peel, could not come. He was at the House of Commons, steering through Parliament the controversial Bill to repeal the Corn Laws. He sent a letter expressing regret at being unable to attend, and mentioning that the Queen had granted Mrs. Haydon a pension of fifty pounds a year from the Civil List. Peel asked for his name to be put down for one hundred pounds as a contribution from his private purse, and Lady Peel assigned a pension of twenty-five pounds a year out of a fund over which she had control.

The meeting resolved that "without presuming to offer any judgment as to the place which Mr. Haydon will ultimately fill in the annals of his art, or any opinion on the controversies in which he was sometimes engaged, this meeting feels that the efforts of his genius, and the circumstances of misfortune which obstructed them, justify an expression of public sympathy with his widow and daughter. That such expression would be most fitly conveyed by securing a permanent provision to his wife and daughter, left wholly destitute by his death; and that a public subscription be opened for that purpose". A considerable sum was subscribed on the spot, and the total of two thousand pounds was reached within two months. By the manner of his death, Haydon achieved what he had failed to accomplish with his exhibition: he had gained the sympathy and support of the public.

Among Haydon's friends no one was more horrified at the tragic outcome of Tom Thumb's competition than Elizabeth Barrett. The victory of the dwarf obsessed her. She had heard the news of Haydon's death at her home in Wimpole Street. Miss Barrett had never met Haydon, and it was nearly two years since they had had a correspondence of a few months. In her letters she had tried, gently and patiently, to understand his grievances. She had broken off the correspondence because she had begun to doubt the wisdom of giving him too much sympathy. She had not heard from him for a year and a half until the week before his death, when he had written to ask for a shelter for five pictures and three trunks containing his private papers.

At the time of Haydon's death Elizabeth Barrett's personal affairs were in a state of crisis. She was planning to elope to Italy with Robert Browning at the end of the summer, a tremendous undertaking for a semi-invalid in her fortieth year. Their plans were secret because her father, whose over-possessive love for her manifested itself in an obsessive concern about her health, would not allow her to marry.

The more Elizabeth Barrett thought about Haydon's suicide, the more she was inclined to conclude that financial problems had been merely an additional irritation, and that his despair had its roots in disappointed ambition. On Friday, 26 June she wrote to Browning, "The cartoon business and his being refused employment in the Houses of Parliament—*that* was bitter: and then came his opposition with Tom Thumb and the dwarf's triumph—he talked bitterly of *that* in a letter to me of last week . . . He was a man you see, who carried his whole being and sensibility on the outside of him; nay worse than *so*, since in the thoughts and opinions of the world. All the audacity and bravery and self-exultation which drew on him so much ridicule were an agony in disguise—he could not live without reputation, and he wrestled for it, struggled for it, *kicked* for it, forgetting grace and attitude in the pang. When all was vain, he went mad and died. Poor Haydon!"

During these days Elizabeth Barrett could not drive the thought of Haydon's suicide from her mind, and in her letters she referred to it again and again. "Poor, poor Haydon," she wrote to a friend. "See how the world treats those who try too openly for its gratitude! 'Tom Thumb for ever' over the heads of the giants." She was convinced that Tom Thumb had played an important part in Haydon's tragedy, and she expressed this belief in a letter to Miss Mitford: "And be sure that the pecuniary embarrassment was not what sank him. It was a wind still more east: it was the despair of the ambitions by which he lived, and without which he could not live. In the self-assertion which he had struggled to hold up through life he went down into death. He could not bear the neglect, the disdain, the slur cast upon him by the age, and so he perished. The cartoon disappointment, the grotesque bitterness of the antagonism of Tom Thumb: these things were too much—the dwarf slew the giant. His love of reputation, you know, was a disease with him; and, for my part, I believe that he died of it. That is my belief."

Some of Haydon's friends differed from Miss Barrett in their opinions of the importance of the part played by the dwarf in the painter's downfall. Some believed that Haydon had been driven to take his life by an accumulation of misfortunes—his failure to win a prize in the Cartoon Contest, the neglect of his exhibition by the public and the overwhelming debts he had no hope of paying. They believed that Tom Thumb was only the last straw. But Elizabeth Barrett was probably nearer the truth in her conviction that the dwarf's triumph had been the main cause of Haydon's despair. Failure, neglect, even the debtors' prison, all these he could have borne; but he could not live without his reputation, and Tom Thumb had taken that from him. During the last few weeks of his life Haydon must have realised that his "day of glory" would never dawn; that his name would be for ever linked to that of a dwarf; and that down the years people would speak not with reverence of Haydon and Raphael or Haydon and Michelangelo but with derision of Haydon and Tom Thumb.

Meanwhile Tom Thumb had left London for a series of farewell performances in the provinces. The abuse in the Press over the part he had played in Haydon's tragedy had no effect on his popularity. Indeed, the crowds that now came to see him were larger than ever. The publicity Tom Thumb was getting was not of Barnum's choosing; it did not show either of them in a good light. But it did result in greater profits, and so confirmed what

Barnum had long believed: that any publicity was better than none and that it did not matter what the newspapers said about you so long as they mentioned your name.

On 4 February, 1847, Barnum and Tom Thumb, accompanied by the dwarf's parents and tutor, embarked on board the *Cambria* at Liverpool. They were returning to New York. Tom Thumb was escorted to the steamer by a great procession of people in carriages, on horseback and on foot. He was followed by a brass band. Many people had come from London especially to see him off. As the dwarf went on board the crowds cheered and sang "For He's a Jolly Good Fellow". Tom Thumb was returning in triumph, like Pompey, Julius Caesar and Scipio Africanus, with enhanced prestige, coffers filled with gold and a vanquished country behind him.

Chapter Eight

YANKEE DOODLE KEEPS IT UP

WITHIN A few days of arriving in New York, Tom Thumb was on show at the American Museum on Broadway. Great crowds came to see him. The monarchs he had met, the palaces and great houses he had visited had increased his interest in the eyes of Americans. As Barnum had remarked to Albert Smith at Warwick Fair, "There's nothing like a bit of state or aristocracy to catch a Yankee with all his talk." So Tom Thumb was advertised as being under the patronage of "all the crowned heads of Europe."

The New Yorkers stared at Tom Thumb in his court dress as though he were a creature from another world. They listened open-mouthed as he talked in a familiar manner of Queen Victoria, Prince Albert and King Louis Philippe. They gaped at the magnificent presents given him by his royal admirers. Ladies queued in endless lines to kiss the little cheeks on which the lips of monarchs had lately lingered.

After a triumphant four weeks at the American Museum, Tom Thumb went for a short holiday to his home town of Bridgeport. There was a great welcome for "little Charlie Stratton" from his friends and neighbours. They had never thought when they had seen him playing in the streets that he was destined to walk with kings. "How old are you now, General?" they asked him slyly, for everyone in Bridgeport knew his true age to be nine. "As Mr. Barnum makes it out, I'm fifteen," Charlie replied with a wink. They admired his smartness, his polished conversation, his knowledge of French. They marvelled at his elegance and exquisite manners. He was now a man of the world, quite changed from the country child they had known. As one of the leading citizens put it, "We never thought Charlie much of a phenomenon when he lived among us, but now that he has become 'Barnumised' he is a rare curiosity."

Barnum told the people of Bridgeport, "The General left America three years ago a diffident, uncultivated little boy; he came back an educated, accomplished little man. He has seen much and profited much. He went abroad poor and he came home rich." Tom Thumb was certainly rich. In Europe he had exhibited before three million people. The gross receipts of his exhibitions, including his theatrical performances and his private appearances at the palaces and houses of the nobility, exceeded £150,000. As Barnum calculated, £150,000, reckoning 56 sovereigns to the pound avoirdupois, equalled 2,678 pounds weight of gold and, as the dwarf weighed only 15 pounds, it followed that he had received 178 times his own weight in gold. Since their agreement of 1 January, 1845, Barnum and Tom Thumb were equal partners, the dwarf taking half the profits.

After a month's rest at Bridgeport Barnum arranged that Tom Thumb and his parents should tour the United States for a year, sharing the profits equally as in Europe. The tour was another triumph for the dwarf. From Buffalo in the north to New Orleans in the south, he drove through the streets of every city in the Union in his tiny carriage with the Shetland ponies, his driver and footman dressed in stockings, breeches, buckled shoes, cocked hats and powdered wigs. In Washington he was received at the White House by President Polk. In Baltimore he was given the freedom of the city. In Philadelphia his levees were crowded with fashionable people. In Boston the progress of his carriage was halted by the crowds that blocked the streets. Loyal Americans everywhere were proud that their republic had produced a dwarf who was the envy of all the decadent monarchies of Europe.

In May, 1848, Tom Thumb and his entourage reached Pittsburgh, and here Barnum decided to leave the tour. He no longer thought it essential to travel with Tom Thumb. He had reliable agents who could exhibit the dwarf competently without his assistance. He preferred to relinquish part of the profits of the tour rather than continue as a travelling showman, and the profits to date were considerable. The daily expenses were never more than thirty dollars, and at Providence the receipts for one day had been almost one thousand dollars. He was glad he was now rich enough to stay at home with his wife and family. For more than four years he had wandered through Europe and America. He was determined that no amount of money would tempt him to leave home again. At Pittsburgh he turned his face to the east, longing to feast his eyes on the gleaming domes and minarets of Iranistan, his new home, which was nearing completion at Bridgeport, Connecticut.

Barnum had chosen Bridgeport as his home because he wanted to live out of New York yet within easy reach of the American Museum. Bridgeport was an ideal situation: the New York and New Haven Railroad ran through the town and there was a daily steamboat service to New York. On a visit from Britain he had purchased seventeen acres of land one mile from the town, with a fine view over Long Island Sound. Always with an eye to business, he decided to build a house in a style so novel that it would serve as an advertisement for the American Museum. He knew he had found what he wanted when he visited Brighton and saw the Royal Pavilion erected for George IV. He had a London architect draw up plans for a house modelled on similar lines.

The building of Iranistan was begun while Barnum was abroad and continued during his American tour with Tom Thumb. The house was a bizarre combination of Hindu and Moorish architecture. The front was one hundred and twenty-four feet long and three storeys high. The roof was surmounted by bulbous domes and slender minarets.

In November, 1848, Barnum took possession and held a house-warming for one thousand guests. They approached the house through an elegant iron gate, down a magnificent avenue, past splendid fountains set in ornamental gardens, with reindeer and elk grazing among the trees. Barnum had transplanted hundreds of full-grown trees to give his gardens an effect that would otherwise have taken a generation to achieve. When his guests saw Iranistan they marvelled. So exotic a building had never before been seen in America.

The interior was a reproduction of all that Barnum had admired in the palaces and great houses of Europe. Niches in the staircase held marble statues from Florence. In the drawing room the walls were decorated with panels representing the Four Seasons. In Barnum's private study the walls and ceiling were hung with orange satin. On the first floor was a long picture gallery. The main room on the second floor was designed as a music and dancing salon and opened on to a balcony commanding a beautiful view over Long Island Sound. The bathrooms were fitted with hot and cold showers.

Barnum was happy at Iranistan. His wanderings were over. He was reunited with his wife and family. He could now devote himself to the great ambition of his life: to make the American Museum the biggest and best of its kind in the world. Since purchasing the Museum six years earlier, he had worked constantly to make it "the town wonder and town talk". Throughout his travels in Europe he had always been on the lookout for new attractions. In Paris he had bought Robert Houdin's automaton writer and a panorama of Napoleon's funeral. In London he bought the celebrated Chinese Collection and had copies made of the machines in the Royal Polytechnic Institution. He had attempted to buy Madame Tussaud's Waxworks. The papers had been drawn up, but the project fell through at the last minute. He was thwarted also in his efforts to buy Shakespeare's House. He planned to move this to New York, but when his scheme had become known there had been a public outcry. Barnum had good reason to regret that he had failed to complete the deal, for rather than allow the house to leave the country the Shakespearian Association would have bought him off with twenty thousand pounds. He had failed also in his attempt to buy the tree on which Lord Byron carved his name. He had made an offer of five hundred pounds to Colonel Wildman, who owned Byron's estate, but the Colonel had flown into a rage at what he considered to be Barnum's Yankee impudence.

In *Sights and Wonders in New York*, a pamphlet published in 1849 to advertise the American Museum, Barnum could describe it as "this magnificent establishment, embracing among its six hundred thousand curiosities, all that is rare and wonderful in the world of nature, or unique and striking in the world of art". And still he thought of ways of improving it. He doubled the space devoted to the permanent collection. He enlarged the Lecture Room to a seating capacity of three thousand. Here performances were held every afternoon and evening. On public holidays as many as twelve separate performances were given. The uniform charge of admission to both the permanent collection and the performances was twenty-five cents, children half-price.

"Moral Drama" was the principal attraction in the Lecture Room. This appealed to the many people who considered theatres to be disreputable. Barnum gave them Biblical plays such as "Moses in Egypt" and temperance plays such as "The Drunkard". They knew they could attend these performances with their children without fear of being shocked and offended.

Barnum had succeeded in making his Museum the most famous place of amusement and instruction in America. The annual number of visitors was greater than that of the British Museum, even though, as Barnum was fond of pointing out, people had to pay to enter his Museum, whereas entry to the British Museum was free. But still he was not satisfied. He dreamed of an exhibition that would excite universal attention and make him and his Museum known and admired throughout the whole world.

He conceived a grandiloquent plan for a "Congress of Nations", nothing less than an assembly of representatives of all races. He meant to secure a man and woman, as perfect as possible, from every people, civilised and barbarous, on the face of the earth. In 1849 he was definitely making preparations for this exhibition when he thought of another enterprise that would achieve the same purpose with far less trouble and much more chance of making money. He decided to bring Jenny Lind to America.

At the time Jenny Lind was the most idolised singer in Europe. This Swedish soprano had impressed such composers as Meyerbeer, Chopin, Berlioz, Wagner and Schubert. The critics of many countries had exhausted the art of eulogy. Jenny was not only the greatest singer of her time but her private life was the model of virtue. Clergymen praised her goodness to the skies, the profane world of theatregoers was awed by her sanctity, and enormous prices were paid to hear her sing. She was a plain-featured girl of twenty-nine, but when she sang her face became transfigured and shone like that of an angel.

Three months after Barnum's departure from Britain she had taken London by storm. The Tom Thumb fever had scarcely died down when the Jenny Lind mania began. She arrived in London after a triumphant tour of Europe. At Stuttgart the students had ripped apart the sheets from her bed. At Vienna they had unharnessed her horses and drawn her carriage through the streets. There was the same enthusiasm in London. After Jenny's début the Queen threw a bouquet at her feet. *Punch* named her "the Swedish Nightingale".

Barnum was ready to engage Jenny Lind on any terms. He was even willing to lose money in order to bring the greatest soprano in the world to America. He reckoned that such an enterprise could bring nothing but credit both to himself and to the American Museum. His terms were the highest ever offered to a singer.

Jenny was to appear in one hundred and fifty concerts for one hundred and fifty thousand dollars. He was to pay all the travelling expenses not only for Jenny herself but also for the maid, the dresser and the secretary who were to accompany her.

When Jenny Lind agreed to Barnum's terms she must have wondered how he proposed to make the enterprise pay. Barnum himself tells us that she had been warned against him by assurances that he was "a humbug and a showman, and that, for the sake of making money by a speculation, he would not scruple to put her in a box and exhibit her through the country at twenty-five cents a head". But she could not resist such an enormous amount of money. She was also attracted by the prospect of visiting the New World.

Barnum knew that so great an outlay could not be covered by the mere display of Jenny's vocal talent. He was basing his hopes of success not only on her merits as a singer but also on her reputation for goodness. He believed that thousands of Americans would go to her concerts for this reason alone.

Although Jenny Lind was the toast of Europe, her name was scarcely known in America; but so skilfully did Barnum manipulate the New York Press that the interest of the public had reached fever pitch by the time she was due to arrive. He had boosted her as much for her benevolence as for her singing, and music lovers formed but a tiny minority of the great crowd that welcomed her when she landed in New York on 1 September, 1850.

The excitement of the New Yorkers was unbounded and did not die down for weeks after her arrival. Tickets for her first concert were sold by auction. The first man to buy a ticket was a hatter, and this distinction was to make his hats famous throughout the Union and make him a very rich man. A thousand tickets were sold on the first day of the auction at an average price of ten dollars. At Jenny's first concert the audience were completely carried away by her singing, and Barnum declared that at that moment he would not have taken two hundred thousand dollars for his share of the profits in the enterprise. By the end of Jenny Lind's American tour he was to net considerably more by continuing to pull "at the heart-strings of the public preparatory to a relaxation of their purse-strings". Wherever she went he made certain that everyone knew of her charity. Whether the donation was five dollars or five hundred, all found their way into the newspapers. Even those who did not care for music came to Jenny's concerts just to gaze upon this object of goodness.

Barnum had every reason to be proud of the Jenny Lind enterprise. Not only did he make a colossal profit but the whole affair placed him before the public in a new light. Jenny Lind was the greatest artiste ever to tour the New World. He had shown that his talents extended beyond the exhibition of dwarfs. Not that he had forgotten Tom Thumb. In 1849 he had organised a big travelling show with the dwarf as the star attraction. "Barnum's Great Asiatic Caravan, Museum and Menagerie" toured the country for four years making huge profits.

Throughout 1854 Barnum sat at his desk in his satin-lined study at Iranistan writing the story of his life. Since the Jenny Lind tour had ended in 1851 he had spent most of his time at Iranistan. During the previous three years he had begun to diversify his business interests. He had become part owner of a steamship, invested in an illustrated newspaper and promoted a fire extinguisher. He was also deeply involved in an extensive property development at Bridgeport. The American Museum was still his chief concern, but this was running smoothly and taking up less of his time. Although he went frequently to New York, he never stayed away from home for more than a day or two.

At Iranistan his day began at seven. He spent the morning in his study, conducting his business affairs. There was always a great pile of letters awaiting him, most of them from strangers eager to put before him their plans for making money. Hundreds of patent rights were offered to him, the owners of which were willing to divide the profits, never less than one hundred thousand dollars and frequently a million, provided the patent was brought out under his name. Innumerable mining and other speculative stocks were offered to him on the same conditions. There was no end to the plans for moneymaking that were continually submitted to him, most of them, in his opinion, "as wild and unfeasible as a railroad to the moon".

Business ended at noon. Before lunch he went for a ride in his carriage, perhaps to visit his farm. He had a keen interest in agriculture, and for a time was president of the local agricultural society. Lunch was followed by a five-minute nap. Most of the afternoon was devoted to his wife and three daughters. In the early evening he took another ride in his carriage. After supper he played cards, preferably with his political cronies. He never lost his taste for politics. He was considered for the Governorship of the state, and was even spoken of as a future President. Guests were not encouraged to stay late at Iranistan. At ten o'clock sharp Barnum went to bed.

Barnum was at peace with himself. Although just forty-three years old, he had already achieved the tranquillity that comes only to the American who knows without doubt that he is a Success. And Barnum was the embodiment of success. He had risen from the poverty of Bethel to the splendour of Iranistan. His name was a household word. He was watched, admired and envied by hundreds of thousands of young Americans anxious to succeed as he had done. He had been urged repeatedly by publishers to write the story of his life. They had assured him that such a book would enjoy enormous sales. The idea appealed to him. He believed that his autobiography would not only make money but would also be an excellent advertisement for the American Museum.

Barnum had led a full and variegated life, which he summarised in the preface of his book in a manner reminiscent of St. Paul: "I have been a farmer's boy and a merchant, a clerk and a manager, a showman and a bank president. I have been in jails and in palaces; have known poverty and abundance; have travelled over a large portion of two continents; have encountered all varieties of men, have seen every phrase of human character; and I have on several occasions been in imminent personal peril."

He wrote of his early life in Bethel. He told how his grandfather, old Phineas, had initiated him into the secrets of smart dealing. He described how he had developed his talents in barter stores, where the customers cheated the storekeeper with their goods, and he cheated the customers with his. He told of his crusading editorship of *The Herald of Freedom*; how he had suffered imprisonment for his liberal views; how he had gone to New York to make his fortune, and the hard times he had endured there before he found his vocation as a showman.

When he wrote of his career as a showman he admitted that he had often deceived the public. He told how he had tricked them with Joice Heth, who was nowhere near the one hundred and sixty-one years he had claimed for her; with the Feejee Mermaid, which was nothing more than the upper half of a monkey sewn to the lower half of a fish; and with Tom Thumb, whose age he had more than doubled. He did not express any penitence for having so often taken money from the public under false pretences. Indeed, he justified himself in a remarkable apologia: "If I have exhibited a questionable dead Mermaid in my Museum, it should not be overlooked that I have also exhibited camelopards, a rhinoceros, bears, orang-outangs, etc., about which there could be no mistake because they were alive; and I should hope that a little 'clap-trap' occasionally, in the way of transparencies, flags, exaggerated pictures, and puffing advertisements, might find an offset in a wilderness of wonderful, instructive and amusing realities. Indeed I cannot doubt that the sort of 'clap-trap' here referred to, is allowable, and that the public like a little of it mixed up with the great realities which I provide. The titles of 'humbug' and the 'prince of humbugs', were first applied to me by my-self."

In 1855 *The Life of P. T. Barnum, Written by Himself* was pub-lished simultaneously in America and Britain. American readers chuckled appreciatively as they read of Barnum's deceptions. They regarded these as being no more than extensions of the tall stories and practical jokes they relished so much. Nor were they shocked or angry when they learned how often Barnum had cheated them. Their only desire was to emulate him, for there was noth-ing they admired more than a smart man. Barnum's "Life" was regarded as a manual on how to become a Success. Reviewers stressed the practical value of the book. "Every young man should read it," the advertisements said. Barnum was praised for his public spirit in so generously revealing to American youth the secrets of his success. Some carping critics complained that these secrets boiled down to nothing more than thrift, temperance and misrepresentation on a large scale, but they were only a small minority. Barnum was also praised for his Christian sentiments. In his book he had been careful always to give God the credit for his success. This mixture of piety and deception gratified many people, especially clergymen, and Barnum's book was often re-commended from the pulpit.

All the honour accorded him by his fellow-countrymen came as no surprise to Barnum. He had never doubted that the world was a better place for his presence. Thinking back over his life, he believed he had "a just and altogether reasonable claim" to be regarded as "a public benefactor, to an extent seldom paralleled in the histories of professed and professional philanthropists".

This claim was bitterly challenged by the British reviewers of Barnum's "Life", especially in the Tory journals. They expressed amazement at his audacity and loathing for his hypocrisy. *Fraser's Magazine* stated that for such a man to be honoured in America attested as no British traveller had ever done to the moral obliquity of that country. *Blackwood's Magazine* declared: "The mendicant, who, on the highway, exhibits sores on his person produced by the application to the skin of a half-penny dipped in acquafortis, and solicits charity on account of his affliction, stands, morally speaking, quite as high as Barnum, who, if one half of his narrative be true, has most richly deserved the treadmill."

Now the reviewers learned for the first time the true age of Tom Thumb. They learned also how Barnum had attacked the British in their weakest point—their snobbish reverence for rank. He told them how shrewdly he had played his cards by wangling an audience for Tom Thumb at Buckingham Palace; and how right he had been in his judgement of the British people, who, because of the Queen's patronage of Tom Thumb, fell over themselves to see the dwarf.

When the reviewers read this they were mortified. The British had always claimed that American republicanism was inferior to their own system of constitutional monarchy. Now Barnum had exposed the folly and weakness of their Queen by showing her slavering over a dwarf and enriching him with presents. "The Thumb tour was the noblest work ever done by an American freeman," *Punch* stated. "It was a death blow at kings and kingships."

For years the British attitude towards Americans had been one of condescension, regarding them as boorish citizens of a fourthrate nation. Now Barnum had avenged all this by showing that the British themselves were even more vulgar and gullible than the Americans. Looking back on Tom Thumb's visit, the reviewers could hardly credit their terrible stupidity. "Where were our brains," *Fraser's Magazine* asked, "that from the palace to the kitchen everyone crowded after the puppet of a Yankee trickster, loading him with presents and with admiration, as if he had been a benefactor of all mankind!"

The reviewers recalled that Tom Thumb's triumphs had taken place under the same roof that had witnessed Haydon's hopeless attempt to regain his reputation and to raise sufficient money to pay his debts. They had often sneered at the Americans for having little appreciation for art, but at least the Americans had never preferred a dwarf to the noblest painter of his generation. For the British to be exposed as vulgar and gullible was hard enough, but, worse than that, in their neglect of Haydon they stood condemned before the civilised world as philistines.

In the advertisements for his exhibition, Haydon had pleaded for the support of the public. Given the choice between the painter and Tom Thumb, they had chosen the dwarf. Tom Thumb's triumph had been the chief cause of Haydon's despair and now his ghost rose up to accuse them. "It is an insanity, a rabies, a madness, a furor, a dream. *I would not have believed it of the English people*."

Barnum had bamboozled the entire British nation, from the Queen downwards, with Tom Thumb. In their anger and bitterness, the reviewers struck at him savagely, as though determined to crush him by the sheer weight of their abuse. They called him the greatest charlatan since Cagliostro. Villains as disparate as Jack Sheppard and Bluebeard were adduced as comparisons. *Tait's Edinburgh Magazine* predicted, "He will ultimately take his stand in the social rank according to testimony of his own producing, and that stand will be among the swindlers, blacklegs, blackguards, pickpockets, and thimble-riggers of his day, and if he soars above them in popular estimation, it will be only from the possession of superior craft and cunning."

The reviewers believed that there was at least one ray of hope in the whole humiliating business: it could never happen again. "Placards may henceforth stun us with their sesquipedalian letters in vain," *Fraser's Magazine* declared; "in vain may the praise of genius re-echo from paragraph and poster. 'Barnumism' all we shall say and pass unheeding by." But this was not to be. Barnum knew, as the reviewers did not, that the mere fact of telling people they had been fools could not make them any wiser. This comprehension of the essential stupidity of mankind was the real secret of his success. By exploiting it he brought advertising and showmanship to a level never before known, and fathered a new race of showmen, advertising men and public-relations men.

While the reviewers attacked Barnum, the British public read his book. Every railway station and bookstall was over-run with library editions, illustrated editions and author's editions. As in America, the book was advertised as a manual on self-help. The public were assured that Barnum had withheld "no rule of life or secret of success". The philosophy of self-help was congenial to the spirit of the times, and Barnum's advocacy of smart dealing as the best and quickest way to make money was to win many supporters in Britain.

Barnum had dedicated his book to "The Universal Yankee Nation". He knew that members of that nation were to be found not only in America but in every country in the world. They were the smart men, the ones who believed that mankind had been divinely ordered into two categories—the outwitters and the outwitted. There were plenty of these men in the competitive, expanding, industrialised Britain of the mid-nineteenth century, as anxious as the Americans to be a Success and as willing to choose Barnum as their guide. It was soon to become apparent that the British had lost more than their American colonies when their army surrendered at Yorktown. When Barnum came to London Yankee Doodle came to town: for better or for worse, the Americanisation of Britain had begun.

FINALE

AFTER READING the British reviews of Barnum's "Life" one would have thought that he would never dare to show his face again in London. But the reviewers had thundered to no effect. Barnum returned to London two years later. His book had sold well in Britain, and he wanted to reap the benefit of the publicity it had given him. He brought with him Tom Thumb and a child actress named Cordelia Howard, who played Little Eva in a dramatised version of *Uncle Tom's Cabin*.

When Barnum arrived in London in 1857 he was penniless. The previous year he had lost all his money through injudicious investments. He no longer owned the American Museum nor Iranistan. His fellow-countrymen, while worshipping Success, did not extend much mercy towards Failure, and the Fall of Barnum had been moralised over by both editors and preachers. The *New York Herald* declared, "All the profits of his Feejee Mermaid, all his woolly horses, Greenland whales, Joice Heths, negroes turning white, Tom Thumbs, and monsters and impostures of all kinds . . . are all swept away, Hindoo palace, elephants and all. It is a case eminently adapted 'to point a moral or adorn a tale'."

In London Barnum was given a great welcome by his friends, among them Albert Smith. Smith had taken to heart all that Barnum had told him on their day out together, and he was now the most successful showman in London, with his long-running Ascent of Mont Blanc entertainment at the Egyptian Hall. Barnum's influence on show business was to be seen everywhere in London. There was not an exhibition that was not advertised as being under some royal or aristocratic patronage, not a theatre manager, actor, singer or musician who did not seek publicity in the Press.

Tom Thumb drew crowded audiences, and Cordelia Howard's Little Eva was a lachrymose success. Barnum left their management to agents while he devoted himself to lecturing. Since the publication of his "Life" he was regarded in Britain as an authority on self-help, and three thousand people crammed themselves into St. James's Hall to hear him speak on "The Art of Money-Getting". Like some Yankee Polonius, the man who had fooled the public with Joice Heth, the Feejee Mermaid and Tom Thumb advised his audience to avoid tobacco, alcohol and debt; to do whatever they did with all their might; to be polite and charitable; never to endorse without security; and, this above all, never to forget that honesty was the best policy. The lecture itself was an admirable example of the art of money-getting, for it was a source of considerable profit to Barnum. During 1859 he delivered it more than one hundred times in London and the provinces.

Barnum returned to America with enough money to pay his debts. He repurchased the American Museum and decorated it with flags, streamers and posters announcing BARNUM ON HIS FEET AGAIN. Now that he was a Success once more all criticism in America was stilled. The second edition of his autobiography, *Struggles and Triumphs*, was even more highly esteemed than the first, telling as it did the story of a man who had fought back against adversity and won.

Tom Thumb continued to exhibit himself, sometimes under his own management and sometimes under Barnum's. The dwarf was growing slowly but surely. By 1861 he had added ten inches to his height, and was eventually to reach a height of forty inches. In 1863 he married Lavinia Warren, another of Barnum's dwarfs. The American public took a tremendous interest in the wedding. For some weeks prior to the ceremony Tom Thumb and his fiancée were on view at the American Museum. The receipts were sometimes more than three thousand dollars a day. It was suggested that Barnum had arranged the match to stimulate business.

In 1864 Tom Thumb and his bride came to London. The Prince of Wales invited them to Marlborough House. Tom Thumb was now portly and pompous, far different from the saucy little fellow who had played with the Prince at Buckingham Palace. In 1869 the Thumbs went on a world tour, which included another visit to Britain.

Tom Thumb and his wife returned to America from their world tour weary of travel. They retired to their home at Bridgeport, a full-sized house, in which they had a suite of rooms furnished to scale. At Bridgeport Tom Thumb devoted himself to pleasure. With every inch he gained he seemed to lose more of his miserliness. Towards the end of his life he was downright extravagant. He owned a steam yacht. He bred racehorses. He smoked expensive cigars. In 1883, at the age of forty-five, he died of apoplexy. Very little remained of the millions of dollars he had earned. The Thumbs had no children, although, to add interest to their exhibition, they had sometimes appeared with a baby, which they claimed to be their own. As a Thirty-Second Degree Mason, Tom Thumb was buried with full Masonic honours. The funeral was attended by ten thousand people, at least eight thousand of whom were women. To the very end Tom Thumb had retained his famous attraction for the ladies.

Barnum came to London for the last time in 1889, when he was seventy-nine years old. Nineteen years earlier he had organised the circus for which he is best remembered—a great travelling show combining museum, menagerie and variety performances. Each year Barnum had made his circus bigger. He added a second ring and then a third. In 1880 he had gone into partnership with James Bailey, owner of a circus almost as large as his own. They combined to form Barnum & Bailey's Circus—the Greatest Show on Earth. In 1889, by a miracle of transportation, this circus came to London.

This time Barnum was worried about his reception in Britain, because seven years earlier he had aroused the anger of the entire nation by purchasing Jumbo and taking him to America. Jumbo, the largest elephant in captivity, had been the favourite animal at Regent's Park Zoo. Barnum had always coveted Jumbo, but he never expected the Zoo to sell him. When, however, the elephant's temper became uncertain, the Zoo let Barnum have him for two thousand pounds.

The announcement of the sale was followed by an outburst of public indignation. Hundreds of letters were written by fathers and mothers whose children had ridden on Jumbo. Letters were received from the children themselves. The Queen and the Prince of Wales begged the Zoological Society not to let Barnum have Jumbo. Some of the Fellows of the Zoological Society brought an action in Chancery for an injunction against the removal of Jumbo. The action failed. *The Times* had a leading article on the decision. Questions were asked in the House of Commons. The American ambassador remarked in a speech that "the only burning question between the two nations is Jumbo". Britain went Jumbo crazy. There were Jumbo hats, Jumbo collars, Jumbo ties, Jumbo soups, Jumbo pies and Jumbo cigars. When there was no longer any possibility of saving Jumbo thousands of sorrowing people visited Regent's Park Zoo to see him for the last time.

Before his visit to Britain in 1857 Barnum had not been worried by the anger of the reviewers, but this time he feared the resentment of the people over Jumbo. The opening night of the circus ended all his fears. Fifteen thousand people crammed Olympia to see the show. Ironically, the climax was the spectacle "Nero and the Burning of Rome", the subject of one of the paintings in Haydon's ill-fated exhibition. But no one thought of Haydon now. Barnum was fêted and dinners were given in his honour. *The Times* declared, "When, in 1889, the veteran brought over his shipload of giants and dwarfs, chariots and waxworks, spangles and circus riders, to entertain the people of London, one wanted a Carlyle to come forward with a discourse upon 'The Hero as Showman'."

At every performance Barnum rode round the arena in an open carriage, smiling benignly. All activity ceased in the three rings. The aerialists swung idly on their trapezes, the clowns stood quietly by. At intervals he would stop the carriage, remove his top hat and call out to the audience, "I suppose you all came to see Barnum, didn't you? Wa-al, I'm Barnum." This was greeted with a roar of "Good old Barnum!"

Two years later, on the occasion of Barnum's death, *The Times* recalled, "There was a threefold show—the things in the stalls and cages, the showman, and the world itself. And of the three perhaps Barnum himself was the most interesting. The chariot races and the monstrosities we can get elsewhere, but the octogenarian showman was unique. His name is a proverb already, and a proverb it will continue." Many years before, on the road from Stratford-upon-Avon to Warwick, Barnum had remarked to Albert Smith, "A man has the right to take in the public if he can. He's fighting single-handed against all creation, and it's the greatest credit to him if he whops them, for they are long odds." Barnum's glowing obituaries in the British Press show the completeness of his victory. He had whopped them all.

BIBLIOGRAPHY

BOOKS AND ARTICLES

American Criticisms on Mrs Trollope's 'Domestic Manners of the Americans'. O. Rich, 1833.

Ames, Winslow. *Prince Albert and Victorian Taste.* Chapman & Hall, 1968.

[Barnum, Phineas Taylor.] *An Account of the Life, Personal Appearance, Character, and Manners, of Charles S. Stratton, the American Dwarf, Known as General Tom Thumb.* Thomas Brettell, 1844.

Barnum, Phineas Taylor. *The Life of P. T. Barnum.* Author's edition. Sampson Low, 1855.

Struggles and Triumphs: or, The Life of P. T. Barnum. Edited, with an introduction, by George S. Bryan. New York, Alfred A. Knopf, 1927.

'Barnum', *Fraser's Magazine*, February, 1855.

Barrett, Elizabeth. *Elizabeth Barrett to Miss Mitford.* Edited by Betty Miller. John Murray, 1954.

Elizabeth Barrett to Mr Boyd. Edited by B. P. McCarthy. John Murray, 1955.

Letters of Elizabeth Barrett to B. R. Haydon. Edited by Martha Hale Shackford. Oxford University Press, 1939.

Letters of Robert Browning and Elizabeth Barrett. 2 vols. Smith Elder, 1899.

The Unpublished Letters of Elizabeth Barrett to Mary Russell Mitford. Edited by Betty Miller. John Murray, 1954.

Barton, Margaret, and Sitwell, Osbert. *Sober Truth.* Macdonald, 1944.

Boase, T. S. R. *English Art, 1800-1870.* Oxford, Clarendon Press, 1959.

Catlin, George. *Letters and Notes on the Manners, Customs and Condition of the North American Indians.* 2 vols. Egyptian Hall, 1841.

Notes of Eight Years Travel and Residence in Europe with his North American Indian Collection. 2 vols. Published by the Author at his Indian Collection, No. 6, Waterloo Place, London, 1848.

Cunliffe, Marcus. *The Literature of the United States.* Penguin, 1954.

Desmond, Alice Curtis. *Barnum Presents General Tom Thumb*. Collier-Macmillan, 1954.

Dickens, Charles. *American Notes*. Chapman & Hall, 1842.
The Letters of Charles Dickens. Nonesuch Press, 1938.
Martin Chuzzlewit. Collected edition. Chapman & Hall, 1844.

Fitzsimons, Raymund. *The Baron of Piccadilly: the Travels and Entertainments of Albert Smith, 1816-1860*. Geoffrey Bles, 1967.

George, Eric. *The Life and Death of Benjamin Robert Haydon, Historical Painter, 1786-1846*. Second edition. With additions by Dorothy George. Oxford, Clarendon Press, 1967.

'The Great American Humbug', *Tait's Edinburgh Magazine*, February, 1855.

Hall, Basil. *Travels in North America in the Years 1827-28*. Whittaker, 1829.

[Hamilton, Thomas.] *Men and Manners in America*. Edinburgh, Blackwood, 1833.

Haydon, Benjamin Robert. *The Diaries of Benjamin Robert Haydon*. Edited by Willard Bissell Pope. 5 vols. Harvard University Press, 1963.

Hayter, Alethea. *A Sultry Month: Scenes of London Literary Life in 1846*. Faber and Faber, 1965.

Hartnoll, Phyllis. *Oxford Companion to the Theatre*. Oxford University Press, 1965.

Hunt, Mabel Leigh. *Have You Seen Tom Thumb?* Philadelphia, Frederick A. Stokes, 1942.

Irving, Washington. *The Sketch Book of Geoffrey Crayon, Gent*. New York, New American Library, 1961.

Johnson, Edgar. *Charles Dickens: his Tragedy and Triumph*. 2 vols. Gollancz, 1953.

Lever, Tresham. *The Life and Times of Sir Robert Peel*. Allen & Unwin, 1942.

London County Council. *Survey of London*. Vols. 29 & 30. *The Parish of St. James. Westminster*. Part 1. *South of Piccadilly*. Athlone Press, 1960.

Longford, Elizabeth. *Victoria R. I*. Weidenfeld & Nicolson, 1964.

McKechnie, Samuel. *Popular Entertainments Through the Ages*. Sampson Low, 1931.

Macready, William Charles. *The Diaries of William Charles Macready*. Edited by William Toynee. 2 vols. Chapman & Hall, 1912.

Masson, David. *Memories of London in the Forties*. Blackwood, 1908.

Maxwell, Sir Herbert. *The Honourable Sir Charles Murray, K.C.B.* Blackwood, 1898.

Miller, Betty. *Robert Browning*. John Murray, 1952.

Murray, Hon. Charles Augustus. *Travels in North America, 1834–6.* 2 vols. Richard Bentley, 1839.

Nevins, Allan. *America Through British Eyes*. New York, Oxford University Press, 1948.

Nicoll, Allardice. *A History of English Drama, 1660–1900*. Volume IV. *Early Nineteenth Century Drama, 1800–1850*. Cambridge University Press, 1955.

Pevsner, Nikolaus. 'Egyptian Revivals', *Architectural Review*, May, 1956.

Planché, James Robertson. *Extravaganzas of Planché, 1825–71*. Edited by T. F. D. Croker and S. Tucker. Volume 2 containing *The Drama at Home*. Samuel French, 1879.

Recollections and Reflections. Sampson Low, 1901.

Reach, Angus Bethune. 'The Disadvantages of Not Being a Dwarf', *Douglas Jerrold Shilling Magazine*, April, 1846.

'Revelations of a Showman', *Blackwood's Edinburgh Magazine*, February, 1855.

Rowell, George. *The Victorian Theatre*. Oxford, Clarendon Press, 1956.

Scott, C., and Howard, C. *The Life and Reminiscences of Edward Leman Blanchard*. 2 vols. Hutchinson, 1891.

Smith, Albert. 'A Go-Ahead Day with Barnum', *Bentley's Miscellany*, Vol. XXI, 1847.

Straus, Ralph. *Sala: Portrait of an Eminent Victorian*. Constable, 1942.

Tietze-Conrat, E. *Dwarfs and Jesters in Art*. Phaidon, 1957.

Trollope, Frances M. *Domestic Manners of the Americans*. 2 vols. Whittaker, 1832.

Vizetelly, Henry. *Glances Back Through Seventy Years*. Kegan Paul, 1893.

Wallace, Irving. *The Fabulous Showman*. Hutchinson, 1960.

Werner, Morris Roberts. *Barnum*. Jonathan Cape, 1923.

Wood, E. J. *Giants and Dwarfs*. Richard Bentley, 1868.

Yates, Edmund. *His Recollections and Experiences*. Richard Bentley, 1885.

Young, G. M. *Early Victorian England, 1830–1865*. 2 vols. Oxford University Press, 1934.

BIBLIOGRAPHY

ANNUALS

Annual Register
Comic Almanack
Littell's Living Age

JOURNALS

Art Union Monthly Journal
Examiner
Illustrated London News
Man in the Moon
Punch

NEWSPAPERS

Daily News
Liverpool Mercury
Morning Chronicle
The Times

INDEX

Albert, Prince, 90, 94, 96, 103, 105, 111, 129, 134
America, British attitude towards, 33–6, 38–9, 41, 44–9, 52, 63–6

Bailey, James, 167
Barnum, Phineas Taylor: birth, 36; formative influences, 36–7; experiences in barter stores, 37–9; organises lottery, 39–40; starts *The Herald of Freedom*, 42; imprisonment and release, 42–4; leaves for New York, 44; difficulty finding work in New York, 50, 52; exhibits Joice Heth, 5–16; exhibits Signor Vivalla, 19–22; organises "Barnum's Grand Scientific and Musical Theatre", 53–5; goes into partnership with Proler, 54–5; buys Scudder's American Museum, 55–6; exhibits the Feejee Mermaid, 27–31; improves the American Museum, 56–8; first meeting with Charles S. Stratton, 58–9; Stratton's parents allow Barnum to exhibit their son, 59–60; exhibits Stratton under the name of Tom Thumb, 60; Tom Thumb's début at the American Museum, 60–2; decides to take Tom Thumb to Europe, 33, 63; sails for Britain, 66–7; arrives in Liverpool, 68–9; exhibits Tom Thumb in Liverpool, 72–3; meets John Medex Maddox, 73; Tom Thumb's début at Princess's Theatre, London, 73–4, 78–9; visits Edward Everett, 80–1; rents Lord Talbot's house in Grafton Street, 82; takes Tom Thumb to Baroness Rothschild's party, 82–3; meets the Honourable Sir Charles Augustus Murray, 83–6; exhibits Tom Thumb at the Egyptian Hall, 86–9; first audience with Queen Victoria, 90–4; second audience with Queen Victoria, 95–6; third audience with Queen Victoria, 97–8; continues to exhibit Tom Thumb at Egyptian Hall, April–July 1844, 93, 102–4; attends the Military Review, 104–5; suggests sight-seeing trip to Albert Smith, 2; visits Stratford-upon-Avon, 16–19; visits Warwick Castle, 22–4; visits Warwick Fair, 24–6; visits Kenilworth Castle, 31; visits Coventry, 32; takes Tom Thumb to Paris, 114–17;